COOL
careers
for
girls

in

HEALTH

Also by the same authors

Cool Careers for Girls with Animals

Cool Careers for Girls in Sports

Cool Careers for Girls in Computers

Cool Careers for Girls in Engineering

Cool Careers for Girls in Food

IMPACT PUBLICATIONS

COOL careers

for girls

in

HEALTH

Ceel Pasternak & Linda Thornburg

Library of Congress Cataloging-in-Publication Data

Pasternak, Ceel, 1932-
    Cool careers for girls in health / Ceel Pasternak & Linda Thornburg.
        p. cm.
    Includes bibliographical references (p.) and index.
    Summary: Profiles eleven women who work as nutritionists, personal
    trainers, doctors, dentists, or other health professionals and explains
    their duties and how they prepared for and got their positions.
    ISBN 1-57023-125-7 (hbk.)—ISBN 1-57023-118-4 (pbk.)
    1. Women in medicine—Vocational guidance Juvenile literature. 2. Allied
    health personnel—Vocational guidance Juvenile literature. [1. Women in
    medicine—Vocational guidance. 2. Allied health personnel—Vocational
    guidance. 3. Vocational guidance.]
    I. Thornburg, Linda, 1949-   . II. Title.
R692.P37 1999
610.69'082—dc21
                                99-26373

                                CIP

Publisher: For information on Impact Publications, including current and forthcoming publications, authors, press kits, bookstore, and submission requirements, visit Impact's Web site: www.impactpublications.com

Publicity/Rights: For information on publicity, author interviews, and subsidiary rights, contact the Public Relations and Marketing Department: Tel. 703/361-7300 or Fax 703/335-9486.

Sales/Distribution: All paperback bookstore sales are handled through Impact's trade distributor: National Book Network, 15200 NBN Way, Blue Ridge Summit, PA 17214, Tel. 1-800-462-6420. All other sales and distribution inquiries should be directed to the publisher: Sales Department, IMPACT PUBLICATIONS, 9104-N Manassas Dr., Manassas Park, VA 20111-5211, Tel. 703/361-7300, Fax 703/335-9486, or E-mail: coolcareers@impactpublications.com

Book design by Guenet Abraham

*Dedicated to the women in this
book who were kind enough to share
their experiences with us in order
to help girls.*

Contents

Careers in health care offer many rewards, including the satisfaction that comes from helping people feel better, from finding new and better ways to fight disease and prevent illness, and from helping bring new life into the world. It was a health care professional who had the pleasure of informing your mom, "It's a girl!"

In the United States, more than four million people work in the health care field. If you choose to explore a career in health, you will find plenty of options, with more than 200 different health care occupations today and new jobs being created as technology changes.

The health care careers in this book focus for the most part on those careers where health professionals work one-on-one to heal sick people and to help people stay healthy. Health is an optimum state of well being, according to Webster's Dictionary, and The World Health Organization expands on that, saying health "is a state of complete physical, mental, and social well-being and not merely the absence of disease or infirmity."

Many people don't think about their health until something happens to it, but from birth and throughout our entire lives, we interact with health care professionals. They practice in schools, in hospitals, in doctors' offices, at fitness or wellness centers, on cruise ships, in the armed services, in patients' homes, in nursing homes, in pharmacies, at work sites, and in laboratories. Some health professionals teach others how to care for people, and some professionals help people who have emotional and mental health problems. Some health professionals focus on preventing violence, and others focus on researching how to

1

stay healthy into old age. Health care is a great field to be in because, wherever you live, jobs are usually available. You can even work outside the United States.

In my own career as a nurse and nurse practitioner, I have known the rewards of working in health care. One day while working, I received a phone call requesting me to meet a woman at the registration desk. As I approached her, she smiled a wide grin and said, "Nadine, It's been so long—God sends us people when we need them." I immediately recognized Mary Ann, an undergraduate classmate. I asked if she was visiting someone. She said no and stated "I have breast cancer. I am the patient."

I was somewhat stunned because she looked vibrant, a healthy 36-year-old woman. I embraced her and said "I am here for you." We had been through so much together—four years at college, her wedding, and the births of her children. Mary Ann was a dynamic singer, with a magnetism that would fill a room. It was tough to watch a woman who had been Miss Howard University weaken. Two years went by—breast surgery, chemotherapy, radiation therapy, and a reoccurrence. We laughed together, we cried together. When she was diagnosed with terminal cancer, we continued to fight, but we also prepared for the end. The last time I saw Mary Ann she was being discharged from the hospital, and in her weakened state she grasped my hand and sang to me the hymn "Amazing Grace." With Christmas a few days away, she told me she planned to hold on. She died December 31, 1997. My personal and professional relationship with Mary Ann will endure forever. Though she was not healed physically, her spiritual renewal and healing were evident. To this day I carry her obituary in my planner as a reminder of her strength and courage. What a privilege and reward as a friend and as a nurse to experience this relationship.

Getting Started Now

This book is a great place to start researching health careers. The stories of the women working in the field provide an overview of educational requirements, a typical day, and the challenges and triumphs of their respective occupations. You will also learn that some women made their career choices when they were girls. Along with each story you will find a checklist with some clues about what type of personality would be suitable for a particular job. Information about salaries and employment opportunities is also provided. The last chapter, Getting Started on Your Own Career Path, gives you advice about what to do now, identifies helpful reading materials and web sites, and lists organizations you may contact for additional information. As you think about a career in health care, consider these ideas:

. . .

Take biology, chemistry algebra, and courses that build your communication skills.

- As you watch television dramas that involve health care, try to identify the different health professionals involved and observe their roles.
- Volunteer at a local hospital. Most hospitals have Junior Volunteer Programs (Candy Stripers). Some schools offer credit for volunteer hours.
- Identify a role model or mentor and work closely with them as you prepare for your career.
- Test the waters early! Some health careers are open to you immediately after high school graduation. Talk to your guidance counselor about local vocational programs in your area, including dental assistant, radiologic technologist, physical therapy assistant, and others.

Make a Difference

Today, women are represented in all health care professions. Two women have recently served as Surgeon General of the United States—the highest government position designed to keep the nation's health agenda on track.

A career in health takes time, dedication, and the willingness to sometimes put the needs of others before your own. If you enjoy being around people and consider yourself a people person, can relate well to others, and like to work on a team, then perhaps a health care career is for you. The most important reason to choose a career in health should be your desire to make a difference. The desire to help a person achieve an optimum state of well-being is a wonderful gift, and it will continue to reward you throughout your career.

COOL
careers
for
girls

in

HEALTH

Marla L. Shuman

Marla L. Shuman, M.D., FCCP (Fellow of the American College of Chest Physicians), Partner, Pulmonary and Critical Care Specialists of Northern Virginia, PC, Annandale and Fairfax, VA

Major in Liberal Arts, master's degree in Biomedical Engineering, M.D. Internal Medicine, Pulmonary Care

Physician in Private Practice

Her Patients Breathe Easier

Marla Shuman spends 10 to 12 hours a day with people. As a doctor of internal medicine with a subspecialty in pulmonary (lung) care, she sees many sick people each day. "I love taking care of people and getting to know so many people. I'm amazed at the things people share with me. It's wonderful."

Marla's day starts about 7:30 in the morning when she arrives at the hospital to visit her patients. While Marla isn't a surgeon, she often assists the surgeon and visits her patients before and after surgery to monitor their care. From the hospital, she drives to her office nearby and starts seeing patients who have

PHYSICIANS

- MD graduates in residency $20,000 to $30,000
- Beginning doctors $28,000 to $36,600
- Average earnings Internal Medicine $125,000

Because of changes in the way healthcare is delivered, physician future earnings may vary depending on organization type and practice.

Source: *Career Information Center* (6th ed.). (1996). New York: Simon & Schuster.

MARLA'S CAREER PATH

Goes with doctor father
▼ on his rounds

High school sports,
▼ girl scouts

Graduates
college
age 19

made appointments. Patients are scheduled for 15-minute visits, and during that short time Marla must check results of laboratory tests, ex-amine the patient, decide upon treat-ment, and then write it all down in the patient's records.

In her office, where Marla works

My parents convinced me that being a doctor would be challenging to me, and that doctors did a lot of counseling, so I stayed on track in pre-med.

Works in doctor's office and as waitress

Studies biomedical engineering, bikes, skis

Gets master's degree

with a receptionist and nurse, big machines hooked up to computers test how well a patient is breathing. Her nurse runs these tests and gives the results to Marla, who uses them to analyze and diagnose each individual's illness.

Marla's patients have lung ailments—from bronchitis or pneumonia to asthma, emphysema, or lung cancer. When patients have diseases that cannot be cured, Marla can offer treatments to help the patient—improve the symptoms, ease breathing difficulties, and help with pain. "I deal with death a great deal," she says. "While I personally have not had a physical illness where there is no hope and there is a lot of suffering, I have felt these experiences intensely by being with my patients. I can relate to the people going through this kind of suffering and comfort them somehow."

Sometimes patients don't want to do what Marla thinks is best for them. "That's when I get to use some creativity to convince patients to do what I believe is the right treatment. For example, I've tried to persuade someone to take exercise classes because it will improve their breathing or to have screening tests and regular checkups to make sure the rest of the body is functioning properly."

Other patients make Marla a part of their life and look to her for guidance and approval. "It's really surprised me," she says. "I get to know things about people that you normally wouldn't get to know if you were just a friend, because they tell you their secrets. It's amazing to me. People don't really need to come to

9

me for approval, but then I realize that I'm important to them. This is one of the things I love about my job."

Marla has to pay just as much at-tention to the business side of being a doctor as she does to caring for her patients. She works with other lung doctors, and they are all partners in

My life is all about **trying to put more stuff in to less time**—seeing more patients, preparing papers and giving presentations to fellow doctors, **serving the community and** my religious groups.

the business, not employees. The partners share being "on call" for their many patients; two of them are scheduled every night to cover any calls or emergencies from 4:30 p.m. until 7:30 a.m. the next morning. Sometimes this means spending long hours at night and then working regular hours the next day.

As business owners, the doctors must spend time running the business. They have to hire and supervise office staff (especially to handle insurance paperwork), nursing staff, accountants, and lawyers. After paying the costs of running the business (people, office space, equipment, and so forth), the partners usually pay themselves a salary and then share any profits or put the money back into the business.

She Follows in Dad's Footsteps

Marla is the middle daughter. She has two older sisters and one younger sister. Her father, now de-

CAREER CHECKLIST ✓

You'll like this job if you ...

- Are willing to study for a number of years for a good income later

- Love to help all kinds of sick people

- Can deal with death and suffering

- Can work long hours

- Are interested in the business side of medicine

- Have good communication skills

GROUNDBREAKERS

The First Women Physicians

In 1849, Englishwoman Elizabeth Blackwell (1821-1916) was the first woman to receive her MD degree in the United States. Convinced that the practice of medicine especially suited women, she persuaded Geneva College in upstate New York to educate her. Her sister Emily also became a physician.

A year later, in 1850, the first American woman to receive her MD (from Rochester Eclectic Medical College in New York) was Lydia Fowler (1822-1879). She became a "demonstrator of anatomy," then professor of midwifery. After the college closed in 1952, she treated women's and children's diseases in private practice.

The first African American woman to receive her MD was Rebecca J. Cole in 1867. She worked with the Blackwell sisters in the slums of New York, and later worked in African American communities in Washington, DC, and Philadelphia.

In 1872, the first Chinese woman to receive her MD (from the University of Michigan in Ann Arbor) was Chi Mai-Yu, also known as Dr. Mary Stone.

Sources: Irene M. Franck & David M. Bromstone. (1995). *Women's World*. NY: HarperCollins. *The Reader's Companion to Women's History*. (1998). NY: Houghton Mifflin. *What Women Have Done* calendar. (1998). Library of Congress.

ceased, was a doctor and her mother still lives in nearby Falls Church, Virginia, where Marla grew up. "From the beginning I was the designated doctor. My sisters felt the pressure to become doctors, but made other choices—one is a lawyer and two are critical care nurses."

Marla and her Dad were very close. He had an internal medicine practice with a specialization in pulmonary care. (After a heart attack, he closed his office and worked part-time at charity clinics.) "He took me with him on his rounds; he shared with me how important medicine was to him. I just assumed I'd be a doctor, and I'd go into practice with him when I grew up."

Marla played basketball, lots of soccer, was a Girl Scout, and had leadership positions in high school. In her early teens, she thought she would be a religious leader and help kids understand the Jewish religion. Her parents persuaded her that she could better help people as a doctor. Later when she was in college working in the career center, she thought

the evening waitressing. I need to be with lots of people."

While waiting to get into medical school, Marla decided to follow her interest in engineering. "I loved physics. I had taken a special college course called physics of the human body. I did a term paper on the function of the kidney, with all the equations and physical explanations. Engineering is the practical application of physics, so I decided to get a master's degree in biomedical engineering."

To get her master's degree, Marla returned to the University of Virginia in Charlottesville. She studied, but also took up skiing at the nearby ski resort and did lots of hiking and biking. After getting her master's degree, she was interviewing for a job in Wisconsin as an engineer when she was accepted to medical school.

she might want to be a counselor. "My parents convinced me that being a doctor would be more challenging to me, and that doctors did a lot of counseling, so I stayed on track in pre-med."

When Marla graduated from college (she was 19), she expected a trip to Europe because some of her friends had received trips to Europe after graduation and because she had been to Israel with the family as a teenager. But her dad was losing someone at his office and she was needed there. "I found it boring because my job was mostly paperwork. I got another job in

8 More Years of Study

It was while she was at medical school, Eastern Virginia Medical School at Norfolk, that her father closed his practice and retired to do

dency, which is the time commitment for a basic residency. (Residency involves working in a teaching hospital, where as a recent medical school graduate she is paid a salary and her work is supervised.) Marla then got a critical care and pulmonary medicine

I enjoy biking, skiing, having fun socializing with family and friends. There's never enough time.

volunteer work. Marla realized she could no longer plan to work with her father. However, a doctor friend of her father's contacted Marla about joining his practice.

Marla finished the 4-year medical school program in 3 years. Then she did a 3-year internal medicine resi-

fellowship and did 2 years (less 3 months) of training. Marla also arranged to work extra hospital coverage rotations at night and on weekends to add to the $22,000 salary she got during her training. As her fellowship was ending, Marla contacted her father's doctor friend back home in Falls Church and began exploring going into practice with him.

"I decided to join him, and we drew up a contract about the salary I would be making and that bonuses would go toward purchasing the practice. He decided to retire after I had been there 3 years. There was more negotiating, solving some of our disagreements, before I actually bought the practice."

Marla worked solo for a while after her employer retired, but realized that she would be better off if she could join with other doctors and share the patient load and all the burdens that come with running a small business. When she approached a doctor group that she knew because they had been covering each other's weekend calls from patients, they were interested and contract negotiations began. Marla has been with that group for 2 years.

Work Hard, Then Play

Marla drives a 10-year-old Acura Legend, but enjoys the "toys" that her high income can provide—like ski equipment, a road bike, exercise equipment—and being able to travel to use her toys. As a single person, Marla makes an effort to get out with friends and family to concerts, plays, and sometimes just to shop, even though she has limited time because of her long hours. When she was introduced (by a friend) to her fiancé, Victor, they talked on the phone every night before they finally met. "We started having dates going to the gym at 4:30 in the morning so that I could go to work at 7:30. That's when I knew he was the one for me. This was real. I told my mother I'd met 'the one.'"

Marla has friends who are doctors. "We have a ladies-night-out group that gets together to unwind. We are all interested in letting girls know what it's like to be a doctor. It's great! We love it."

Stephanie Ferguson

STEPHANIE FERGUSON

Stephanie Ferguson, Ph.D., RN, associate professor, Division of Nursing,Howard University, Washington, DC

Major in Science in Nursing, master's degree in Nursing with focus on Perinatal/Neonatal and Clinical Nurse Specialist track; Ph.D. in Nursing with focus on Health Policy and Multicultural Interventions.

Educator, Clinical Nurse Specialist

A Passion for Women, Children, and Families

From the time she was 5 years old, Stephanie Ferguson wanted to be a nurse. "I love people, and I love caring for people," she says. After a career that has included caring for pregnant mothers and newborn babies, helping set up health care programs to assure that mothers and babies get the best care, and traveling all over the world to give advice on maternal and child care issues, Stephanie has become a professor.

Stephanie teaches nurses who are attending graduate school to become nurse practitioners. Her classes are about nursing theory; how to care for mothers, newborn babies, and young children; and about international health policy. The students come from

UNIVERSITY FACULTY

Full-time nurse faculty, with doctorate degree, salary ranges:

- Assistant Professor, $33,951 to $118,277
- Associate Professor, $26,884 to $150,000
- Professor, $42,520 to $171,791

Source: *1997-1998 Salaries of Instructional and Administrative Nursing Faculty in Baccalaureate and Graduate Programs in Nursing* by Linda E. Berlin, Geraldine Bednash, & Deborah Scott. Washington, DC: American Association of Colleges of Nursing.

Has asthma, decides
▼ to be nurse

Works as
▼ nurses' aide

Becomes RN,
▼ works in newborn
intensive care unit

all over the world and have experience working as nurses. Stephanie also is a faculty advisor. She helps students decide on what courses to take, what to write their thesis on to get their advanced degree in nursing, and how

University in Washington, DC, Stephanie teaches in the Graduate Program of the College of Pharmacy, Nursing, and Allied Health Sciences. She teaches all her classes on Mondays from one o'clock in the after-

Going into the 21st century, nurses will continue to be an integral part of the health care system.

to get the experience they need to get good jobs.

An associate professor at Howard

noon until about nine at night. During the rest of the week she does research, consults with hospitals and

Gets master's, ▼ becomes perinatal outreach educator in public health

Works on Sickle Cell test ▼ for newborns

Ph.D.

Gets Ph.D., research ▼ on teen pregnancy

community organizations to set up maternal and child health care programs, writes and edits articles for journals, and works to develop programs that will help nurses take leadership roles in their jobs and in their communities.

Stephanie does many different things, but they are all connected to her interests in child and maternal health care worldwide and to making the nursing profession stronger.

From the beginning of her career as a nurse, she has had an interest in helping pregnant women deliver healthy babies and in caring for newborn babies who need special care.

From Aide to RN

When she was a girl, Stephanie loved the county nurse at her school. Because she had asthma, she visited the nurse often. She was impressed with how kind Margaret Shields was. "I knew I wanted to be a nurse like that," she says, which meant she would get a college degree.

Stephanie has two younger brothers but no sisters. "My parents could afford to help all of us with college but I wanted

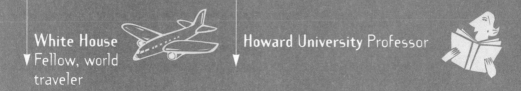

STEPHANIE'S CAREER PATH

White House Fellow, world traveler

Howard University Professor

to do some of it on my own." As a teenager, she volunteered at the hospital in Lynchburg, Virginia, near her hometown of Appomattox, the historic town where the Civil War ended. She liked working with patients so much that she went to the hospital's nursing school and became a nurses' aide. She earned money all through high school and college as a nurses' aide.

When she started college at the University of Virginia in Charlottesville, Stephanie thought she would study Spanish. She wanted to be an interpreter for the United Nations. She had worked with elderly people as a nurses' aide, and, although she enjoyed nursing, she did not think it was the right career for her. But she found out that many of the students in her Spanish classes

also wanted to be United Nations' interpreters. It was a very competitive field to be in! Stephanie's mom, who was one of the first women to work in quality control in the nuclear energy industry, told her that maybe she should think about nursing as a career choice. "You wouldn't have to work with older people; you could specialize in working with women who are pregnant and babies," she said.

So Stephanie began to study nursing, and worked on weekends as a nurses' aide at the University of Virginia hospital to help pay her way through school. In her last year of nursing school, she took courses in maternal and child care because she was interested in this specialty of nursing.

Babies by Night, Books by Day

"I knew from the time I got my B.S. in nursing that I wanted to get a doctorate eventually. I wanted to teach and work at the policy level of health care. I wanted to be involved in helping people who are vulnerable to have a better quality of life."

Once she had her degree, Stephanie got a job as a registered nurse in the newborn intensive care unit of the University of Virginia hospital. She cared for premature and sick babies. Because the University had a program for its employees that helped pay tuition, Stephanie decided to work at night and take classes during the day. She liked the night shift because she could spend more time with the babies, and because she got off at 7:30 in the morning and could spend the day working on her master's degree in nursing.

Stephanie worked on and off for the University of Virginia hospital system for 14 years while she pursued her studies. She thinks the hos-

You'll like this job if you ...

Love kids and moms

Want to improve the well being of others

Are outgoing and can be a leader

Will work and study hard

Can manage projects and set priorities

Love to help others learn

Appreciate differences in people's backgrounds and talents

pital has one of the best intensive care units for newborn babies in the United States and says she learned a lot about how to care for babies from the people who worked there. "I have seen the technology for newborn ba-

There are so many different options in nursing now.

You can work in clinics in health care centers, as a nurse manager, as a nurse consultant, as a nurse anesthetist, or as a clinical nurse specialist, like I did.

You could specialize in mothers and children or in another area such as gerontology (working with the elderly).

bies change dramatically in my career. Now they even have medications they can give to newborns to help them breathe, so they don't have to breathe with the help of a machine."

With her master's degree from the Medical College of Virginia at Virginia Commonwealth University in Richmond, Stephanie was now a clinical nurse specialist who had knowledge and expertise in caring for high-risk pregnant women and newborn babies. Women who have diabetes or heart problems may have more trouble delivering a baby and may deliver a baby who needs special care. Girls who are pregnant at a very young age might not take care of themselves and could have babies who are dangerously underweight or critically ill. Stephanie worked at the Medical College as a perinatal outreach educator. Her job was to train hospital staffs in her region by visiting the hospitals and teaching the doctors and nurses about high-risk pregnancies. She also put together conferences so that doctors and nurses could learn the latest information about caring for high-risk pregnancies and newborn infants who are at risk of dying or having long-term health problems.

Next, Stephanie took a job with the Virginia Department of Health as a public health nurse consultant. She helped to implement a test that would screen newborn babies for Sickle Cell Anemia disorders and other diseases that affect the blood. She worked with state legislators to develop policies and a law that would assure that babies got tested. This was important because if Sickle Cell was detected in a newborn baby, the baby could receive medicine that would help to prevent flu viruses and pneumonia. Today most states require the test for Sickle Cell, but when Stephanie was working at this job it was very new, and some people didn't believe it was necessary to test for it.

GROUNDBREAKERS

The Apgar Birth Score

Virginia Apgar (1909-1974) was a physician and anesthesiologist. She was the first woman full professor at Columbia University medical school and the first full professor of anesthesiology. In 1952 she developed the Newborn Scoring System, a way of quickly evaluating a medical condition to assess whether the infant needed emergency medical attention. It became known as the Apgar score also from the initial letters of the five criteria—appearance, pulse, grimace, activity, and respiration. Apgar also appeared on a U.S. postage stamp.

Source: Irene M. Franck & David M. Bromstone. (1995). *Women's World*. NY: HarperCollins

Hole in Her Heart Fixed

Then Stephanie got a job at Mary Washington Hospital in Fredericksburg, Virginia, helping set up a special care nursery and a labor, delivery, recovery, and postpartum unit. She trained the doctors, nurses, and social workers on how to work in the unit. During this time, Stephanie found out that she had to have heart surgery to correct a small hole in her heart. It took her just four months to recover from the surgery. She designed her own recovery program, which included exercise and eating right as well as time for reflection and prayer. "It was somewhat divine that they didn't find this hole when I was born, because the technology wasn't good enough to operate then, and I would have died. When I was a girl, all the doctors were focused on my asthma, so they didn't pick up my heart murmur. I'm proud that it was a nurse practitioner who first discovered the heart murmur."

When she was well enough,

Stephanie took a job in Richmond as a nurse manager of a newborn intensive care unit and as a temporary director of the maternal and child care program. She opened the labor, delivery, recovery, and postpartum unit for the hospital. It was a relatively were ready to go home. Stephanie supervised 250 employees. She was responsible for providing education about childbirth and breast feeding to prospective parents, and for hiring and evaluating the nurses and others who worked in the unit. "As a nurse

I went into nursing because I have a passion for women and children and families.
That's my whole life, to help people in vulnerable populations to become the best they can.
If you're not healthy in body, mind, and spirit, you can have a hard time making a difference in this world.

new idea—moms and babies could stay in the same room until they manager, you can make really good money. But I had always known that

I wanted to get the doctorate, and I had been accepted in the Ph.D. program at the University of Virginia. I had to postpone school for a year to finish up with the things I wanted to do, but I knew that eventually I would go for the Ph.D."

Teens a Vulnerable Group

Before she returned to school, Stephanie got interested in a Salvation Army Club for boys and girls in Richmond. A friend, who was to give a speech to the club, had asked her to take his place because he was getting married that day. Stephanie found that she really enjoyed the kids and they loved her. So she volunteered at the center a few days a week. After Stephanie got into her Ph.D. program, she was one of 11 people in the country to get a grant from the W.K. Kellogg Foundation to improve the health care of at-risk, vulnerable populations. She chose to help the teen center and organized a coalition of 40 different organizations that put together a teen health education program for the club. Then she became the director of teen programs at the club.

Stephanie's doctorate studies were in nursing, with a focus on health policy. During this time she earned money as a research assistant and taught both undergraduate and graduate students about health care policy, nursing and childbearing, and multicultural issues that impact health care and health care policy. One of her research projects was to study how teenage girls could counsel other teenage girls about avoiding pregancy. Stephanie thought that teenagers would listen to other teenagers more than to adults, and she was right. Her research showed that teenagers who have this type of counseling are less likely to engage in sexual relations at a young age.

When she had her Ph.D., Stephanie got appointed as a White House Fellow to work directly with the U. S. Secretary for Health and Human Services (HHS), Dr. Donna E. Shalala.

She helped HHS develop a national strategy to prevent teen pregnancy, and organized a large conference where many groups discussed how

Dr. Shalala ended, Stephanie got her job at Howard teaching graduate student nurses. Along with her writing and research work, she currently is

> I don't stress over things I can't make a difference in. Faith plays a big part.

> It's okay to be a busy person as long as your work is fruitful; you are making a difference in the world.

best to prevent teens from getting pregnant. She helped prepare testimony for Congress. She also traveled to South Africa, Mozambique, and Panama as Dr. Shalala's representative to participate in international health projects.

After her one-year fellowship with

working to set up a program to teach nurses leadership skills, like negotiating skills, public speaking skills, and coaching and mentoring skills. She believes that nurses will play a huge part in the health care system of the future, and that they need good skills to take a leadership role.

Tiffany Medlin Osborn

Tiffany Medlin Osborn

Tiffany Medlin Osborn, M.D., Resident, University of Maryland Hospitals

Major in Biology, M.D. University of Texas Medical School Health Science Center, San Antonio

Emergency Medicine Physician

Critical care with a heart

To Tiffany Medlin Osborn, the most important part of being a doctor is making a difference in a patient's life—being there when someone is hurt and scared, providing medical care and emotional reassurance.

Tiffany is completing her education and is in residency in Emergency Medicine with the University of Maryland hospital system. In less than two years, she'll be an attending emergency room (ER) physician. Even though she currently works 12-hour days seeing patients in ER and sometimes feels like there is no extra time for anything when she is work-

PHYSICIANS

• MD graduates in residency $20,000 to $30,000

• Beginning doctors $28,000 to $36,600

Because of changes in the way healthcare is delivered, physician future earnings may vary depending on organization type and practice.

Source: *Career Information Center* (6th ed.). (1996). New York: Simon & Schuster.

TIFFANY'S CAREER PATH

ing (she barely has time to go to the bathroom), she always tries to be kind to the people she treats and to make them feel less scared about being in the emergency room.

A Typical 12-Hour Day

On a typical day, Tiffany will start at 7:00 a.m. and work until about 7:00 at night. Generally she works five or six days a week, but when she becomes an attending physician she probably will work 12-hour shifts only 3 days a week. One of the reasons she chose emergency medicine is that eventually it will allow her to spend more

time at home. "I want to have time to devote to a family," she says.

Today, Tiffany's first patient is a woman who has a fever of 103 and can't keep any food in her stomach. The woman has no insurance. She got really sick before she saw a doctor and so ended up with pneumonia, after which she had to have her right

Graduates college

Gets accepted into medical school

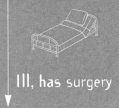

Ill, has surgery

lung removed. Her current sickness is a complication from that surgery. Tiffany has to intubate the woman

air, another member of her team gets the woman admitted to the hospital.

Tiffany moves on to the next patient—a man just brought in by ambulance. The man is sweaty and pale, and he's breathing hard. Tiffany suspects a heart attack. She and her ER team (an attending nurse and technician) do an EKG (electrocardiogram test that shows how the heart is working) and then shock the heart so that it will start pumping well again. The man is in great pain, and Tiffany administers a drug to calm him. Then she moves on to the next patient, a woman who is bleeding from a miscarriage. She has to be sure this woman isn't losing so much blood that her life is in danger. Tiffany has to get the woman admit-

(stick a tube down her throat and into her one lung and hook the tube up to a machine to help the woman breathe). After Tiffany has made sure the woman can breathe and is not in danger of dying from lack of

Meets Jeff Osborn (Ozzy)

Gets residency in Emergency Medicine, marries Jeff

ted to the obstetrics ward of the hospital. The entire day is non-stop emergencies.

Emergency resident doctors at the University of Maryland travel to different hospitals within the university's health care system to get different types of work experience. Tiffany may be working at one of two hospitals in the center of Baltimore where the University's medical

internal medicine, and treating shock and trauma. She also spends lots of time in the hospitals' emergency rooms.

While the ER is very intense—with a steady stream of new patients who need attention—shock-trauma duties can be a combination of fast-action, then slow periods when doctors wait for patients to be brought in. Usually shock-trauma rotations are

Integrity is doing the right thing when no one else is around. (Ozzy's quote Tiffany tries to live by.)

school is located, a hospital in Washington, DC, or at the shock-trauma unit in Baltimore. She is assigned to various "rotations" so she can learn about such things as delivering babies, treating patients who have complications from recent surgeries,

"on call;" the resident works a 24-hour period. During the morning rush hour, lots of accident victims arrive at the ER. One day Tiffany had to care for a military officer with a broken pelvis, who had been hit by a drunk driver while on the way to work. This person also was unconscious from hitting the steering wheel. Tiffany and the trauma team had to make sure the patient was intubated immediately to help breathing, and then stop the bleeding. If the bleeding went into the pelvis, the officer could die.

As the officer was being stabilized and rays were being taken, a victim from another accident was brought in. Her legs were crushed. There was no skin left and the muscles and bone were visible. As Tiffany lifted one of the patient's legs, she could see the bone was in two pieces. Lines (small tubes) had to be put into the patient's veins to stabilize her blood pressure so that her heart could deliver enough blood to her brains and vital organs. Antibiotics had to be given to stop infection. She had to be intubated.

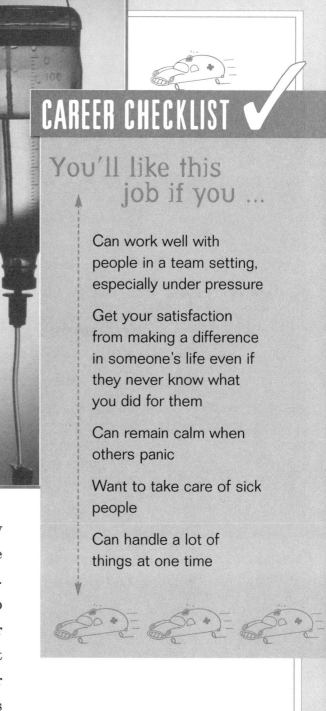

CAREER CHECKLIST ✔

You'll like this
job if you ...

Can work well with people in a team setting, especially under pressure

Get your satisfaction from making a difference in someone's life even if they never know what you did for them

Can remain calm when others panic

Want to take care of sick people

Can handle a lot of things at one time

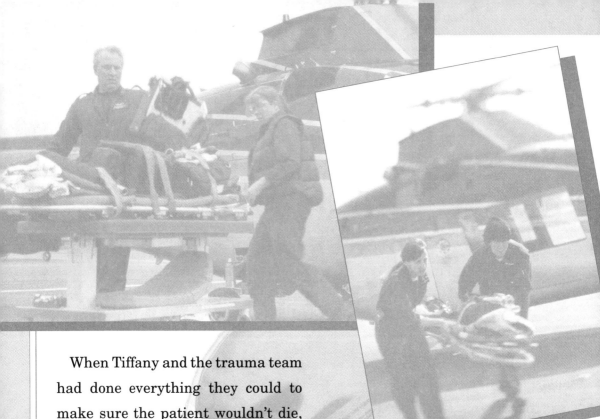

When Tiffany and the trauma team had done everything they could to make sure the patient wouldn't die, they had to rush to another set of accident victims arriving by helicopter—a mother and her little girl. The girl, who had been wearing her seat belt, was basically okay, but the mother, who had not worn her seatbelt, had several broken bones. Tiffany had to check the mother's airways and breathing to be sure that a bone had not punctured a lung, check circulation to make sure the heart was able to pump blood, and because the mother's blood pressure was low, put in lines to help direct blood to the body's organs.

In shock-trauma, Tiffany and her five teammates on call—and an attending physician—are there after everyone else leaves for the day to take care of any patients who spend the night at shock-trauma and any new ones that arrive. In the ER, Tiffany and her team of one other resident and one attending physician care for between 40 and 60 people during a 12-hour shift. An attending physician is in charge in both the ER and shock trauma settings. Resi-

Everyone who comes into the emergency room, no matter where they are from, has one thing in common. They are scared. **They need someone they can believe in**; someone they can trust to take care of them in the best possible way.

They need to be **healed from the inside out,** as one of my patients once said.

GROUNDBREAKERS

Breast Cancer Research

M. Vera Peters, MD, conducted a study showing that those receiving a treatment called lumpectomy (removing a lump) survived as well as those receiving mastectomies (removing entire breast). A graduate of Toronto medical school in 1934, she became a world class radiotherapist/oncologist. She was appointed to the Order of Canada in recognition of her extraordinary contributions to the treatment of Hodgkin's disease and breast cancer. April 10, 1967, the *Journal of the American Medical Association* published her article on the outcomes of the 1935-1960 study of 825 women breast cancer patients.

Source *The Reader's Companion to Women's History*. (1998). NY: Houghton Mifflin

dents have to inform the attending physician about the diagnosis they make and treatment they give. If residents are unsure how to treat a patient, they ask the attending doctor for help. Sometimes the doctor may recommend that residents try things they haven't thought of. In this way, the attending physician supervises the care, but the residents actually treat most of the patients.

Loved Biology, Anatomy, and Literature

Tiffany didn't know she wanted to be a doctor until she was half way through college. As a girl, two of her favorite subjects were biology and anatomy, but she also enjoyed reading literature and poetry. She thinks her exposure to good literature makes her a better doctor. "You can't be a good physician without science, but you can't be a good physician with just science either," she says. "By reading stories or poems, you gain insight into how other people feel, and that helps you gain insight into yourself. Part of being a good doctor is understanding what your patient is feeling and being compassionate. Literature helps you do that."

Another reason Tiffany can be compassionate is because she herself got lots of compassion and support as a girl growing up in Houston, Texas. Tiffany thinks she has the best family in the whole world. Her dad, a history teacher turned fireman, and her mom, an elementary school teacher, gave her lots of support. Tiffany played softball and was on the swim team from the time she was about 9 years old. Both of her parents attended all her games and acted as coaches and scorekeepers for the team. They have been there when she's needed them throughout her life.

Medical School Calls

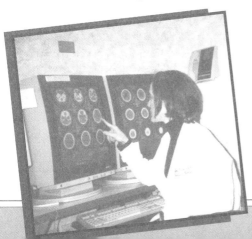

During Tiffany's first year of college, at the University of Houston, she lived at home with her parents and her two younger brothers. But in her sophomore year, she wanted to be on her own to establish her independence. Her parents helped as much as they could, but Tiffany worked two jobs to put herself through school. At one point she and a friend started their own business arranging events and parties for different orga-

If you want to be a physician, you have to do it because you want to take care of sick people and make a difference in their lives, not because of money.

nizations. One of their clients was a modeling agency in Scotland and another was an embassy of a Central American country. When the work became too all consuming, Tiffany knew she had to make a choice—either stay in school or quit and devote her time to the business. She chose to stay in school, because by this time she had decided she wanted to go to medical school after college.

Tiffany's decision to attend medical school was strengthened when her grandmother got sick. Tiffany was very close to her father's mother, who had been a nurse. Her grandmother was dying from a form of Lou Gehrig's disease—a fatal disease of the nerves that weakens all of the body's muscles. Tiffany scaled back her college studies for a semester and spent a lot of time at the hospital. By this time her grandmother was so ill she couldn't even speak.

One doctor who was caring for her would enter the room and just glance at her chart, never stopping to speak entered the room. This doctor did everything he could to make her grandmother comfortable. "He knew

In the emergency room, everybody helps you get your job done. If you are a difficult person, you won't get things done as quickly as they need to be done because people won't want to work with you.

to her, and treating her as if she were already dead. But another doctor, a resident, rated a smiley face drawn by her grandmother every time he he couldn't cure her and she was never going to leave the hospital, but he wanted to care for her anyway. He was kind to her and that made a big impression on me. I think that's when I really decided to be a doctor."

Once the decision was made, there was no stopping Tiffany. Her mother was worried that the life of a physician would be too difficult. She tried to convince Tiffany to study for a physician's assistant job, but Tiffany wouldn't hear of it. "We come from a long line of strong women, and my mother was just doing what she thought was best for me, but I insisted. I wanted the responsibility and control that goes with being the doctor."

It Wasn't Easy

It took two tries at the medical school exam before Tiffany was finally accepted to medical school. After doing poorly on the exam, she took a course that helped her prepare for the exam, which has lots of questions on chemistry, statistics, biology, and a reading comprehension section. She also cut back on her work so that she could devote more time to studying. The next time she took it she passed with flying colors and was accepted into the medical school at San Antonio. But her loan application got misplaced and she had to start medical school without any money, so she worked some odd jobs.

"I would not recommend that anyone work while in medical school," she says. Her mother and father came to visit during her period of extreme poverty and saw that her refrigerator contained a half a carton of milk and two pieces of moldy bread. Her mother was not happy. The family went grocery shopping. Then, when her mother got home, she called a state congressman and complained. "They've lost my daughter's loan application and I want it found," she told the congressman. "Otherwise you won't be getting our vote the next time." The application was found within two weeks and Tiffany got her money.

Her first year in medical school, Tiffany was diagnosed with cancer and had to have surgery. Fortunately, the surgery cured her, and she could get back into school fairly quickly. But because of the surgery, she had to repeat her first year in medical school. Until her third year, along with people and to work well on a team. I got top-of-the-line evaluations in my clinical rotations. I could go into a hospital and get the job done. I read constantly, learned

The amount of money you can make is changing every day. Sure you need to make a living, but money should never be the first reason to become a doctor.

she was about the middle of her class in terms of grades and scholastic performance. But in her third year, she really began to shine. That was when students had to begin doing more clinical work.

"Because of my work experience throughout college, I knew how to get from my seniors, and did my work. I made other people's jobs easier. If you can do that, you will do well."

Right about this time she met her husband, Jeff Osborn (who friends call Ozzy). It was at a friend's wedding and Ozzy had come from Virginia to San Antonio to attend. After the wedding there was some dancing. Tiffany was seated at a table with another man and Ozzy whispered something in the man's ear. Then he went to the other side of the room and looked at his watch. In a little while he was back, standing behind the floor, Ozzy told Tiffany that he had told her companion he had exactly one minute to ask Tiffany to dance, or Ozzy would. Ozzy swept Tiffany off her feet and they haven't touched the ground since, she says.

Ozzy and Tiffany began seeing

man's chair. "Miss Tiffany, I do believe I will excuse myself from this situation because Mr. Osborn would like to dance with you," Tiffany's companion said. Out on the dance each other, even though he lived in Washington, DC, more than 2,000 miles away. They both knew they had something special. Tiffany started applying for residency positions on the East Coast so she could be near Ozzy. She was delighted to land a residency at the University of Maryland in emergency medicine, in which she had decided to specialize because she could help people who were hurt and scared.

A year after Tiffany and Ozzy met, he proposed. They have been married since July of 1998. Ozzy is an energy analyst for the federal government. Tiffany says he is definitely the man for her. They are both single-minded when they have a goal in mind, and the two of them both have a strong 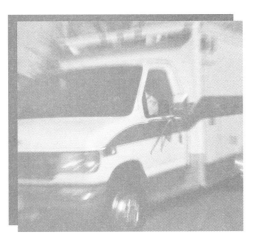 faith in God. They don't have much time together right now, because they both have heavy work schedules, but they enjoy the time they do have and know they will be able to spend more time together in the future, once their careers are more established. For now, they enjoy stealing away to the Virginia mountains, hiking, or just taking a drive to see the leaves change in the fall.

Tiffany spends part of her free time serving on the Board of Directors of the State Chapter for the American College of Emergency Physicians (ACEP), and serving on the Board of Directors for the National Emergency Medicine Residents Association (EMRA). Her position on EMRA includes being a liaison to the Board of Directors of the Council of Residency Directors and to the National ACEP Academic Affairs Committee. She also serves as an advisor to the EMRA national medical student committee and has presented research at two international conferences—Vancouver, Canada, and Oxford, England. She is working to make conditions as good as possible for residents in emergency medicine.

Kim Lerna Kitchen

Kim Lerna Kitchen

Kim Lerna Kitchen, D.D.S, Private Practice, Alexandria, Virginia

Major in Dental Hygiene, D.D.S. Loyola University, Chicago

Dentist

Patients Love Her Chairside Manner

Dr. Kim Kitchen has a great smile (she once wore braces on her teeth). She is a family dentist and has patients of all ages, from 3 to 94. Kim loves her work because she can help people in pain, and she can help people maintain a healthy mouth to prevent pain. She also can make their teeth look better when they smile.

"I had good experiences with dentists when I was a girl. So when it came time to choose a career in the health field, dental hygiene sounded like a great career for me, that's where I started."

Today, Kim has her own business, called a practice. Because of her education—a doctorate in Dental Science—she can do everything from filling a cavity, to surgery, dentures, periodontics (gum care), and even

DENTISTS' TAKE-HOME PAY RANGES:

- less than $100,000   37.0%
- $100,000 to $150,000   27.3%
- $151,000 to $200,000   17.1%
- $201,000 to $250,000   9.4%
- $251,000 to $350,000   6.4%
- $351,000 and up   2.9%

Source: *Dental Practice & Finance's* 1997 doctor compensation survey

DENTAL STAFF SALARIES

Average hourly pay, full-time, 1 to 5 years of experience

- Hygienists $22.33
- Chairside assistants certified (RDA/CDA) $10.32
- Chairside assistants, noncertified $9.63
- Receptionist $11.56
- Business office $10.95

Source: *Dental Practice & Finance's* 1998 staff salary survey

KIM'S CAREER PATH

Plays sports, loves science courses

Graduates college

Job in Florida as hygienist

braces (if she takes special courses). "I'm not restricted to a specialty," says Kim. "I like to do a variety of things."

4-Day Work Week

Kim works only 4 days a week, but the hours are long. She gets to the office at 7 a.m. and gets ready for her day, checking over the scheduled appointments and making sure staff are present and prepared for work. She has two dental hygienists, a dental assistant, and two people who work as receptionists and office staff.

Kim's first appointment is at 7:30 and the last fin-ishes around 4:30, unless there is an emergency patient. She usually sees six to ten patients each day; plus she checks each of the patients that the hygienists are working on. Dentists are encouraged to work no more than 32 hours a week because their work requires strong concentration, good eyesight, and excellent hand-eye co-ordination. However, Kim is "on call" for emergencies, except when she arranges for a fellow dentist to take

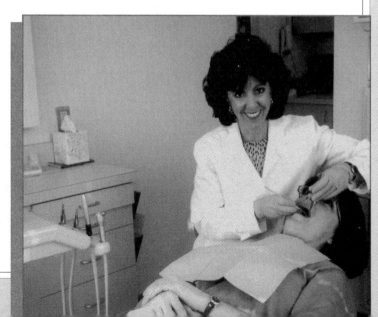

emergency calls, as she does when she travels or goes on vacation.

When Kim is not with her patients, she does paperwork. She pays bills, does payroll, and checks bank and tax records. She calls patients and colleagues and delegates and manages her staff. She is often the last to leave the office, usually about 6 p.m.

"The field of dentistry is really wonderful," says Kim. "We're constantly taking courses, learning new things. I enjoy doing crown and bridge work, which restores teeth and sometimes replaces missing teeth so patients can function better." Kim loves working on children, but likes the variety of patients she has. Most are between 20 and 55. She has some elderly patients who are 80 to 90 years old, and many have their own teeth. But sometimes they can't

chew as well and they don't know what is wrong—Kim can help them.

Kim loves people and likes to get personal with her patients. "Most people hate coming to the dentist," she says, "because there is always fear involved. You have to be able to use psychology with some patients. I like to get to know them. I am constantly adapting to different personalities. It's fun and never gets boring."

Sciences Her Favorite

Kim grew up in St. Petersburg, Florida, where she attended Catholic schools. She and her twin sister, Karen, were cheerleaders and played

KIM'S CAREER PATH

 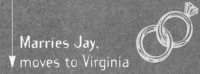
lots of sports—basketball, volleyball, and softball. Kim has two younger brothers. Her father is an artist and musician. When the twins entered high school, Kim's mother worked in their school to help with the expense of having four children in private schools.

Kim earned average grades in school, but enjoyed science courses so much she knew her career would involve the sciences. An older girl at Kim's school was going off to dental hygiene school, and Kim talked with her about the field. "She gave me lots of information. I knew I wanted a health-related field, but I didn't want to be a doctor or nurse and deal with death. Working in hospitals didn't appeal to me. I wanted regular hours, not shift work and always being on call."

Kim also talked with the school counselor. When college representatives came to visit, she learned more about the college dental hygiene programs. "I learned that dental hygienists made good salaries. Most work only 4 days a week, plus there was usually a shortage, so it should be easy to get a job." Kim decided to attend Loyola University in New Orleans, and she entered their 4-year program in Dental Hygiene.

"There are 2-year programs, if you want a quick education and will work strictly for a dentist. But if you are thinking about work in a hospital setting or with a school, or maybe you want to teach, those places want you to have a 4-year degree. I wanted a college degree."

If you aren't sure whether you'd like this type of work, Kim suggests you get a job as a dental assistant. "Technically, dental assistants don't need any formal schooling, they learn on the job. They are there to help the dentist. They have to become certified to take X-rays, but that means taking a weekend course and then passing the test. Some dental students take jobs through a temp agency and learn a lot this way."

Another great thing about becoming a dental hygienist is that you can begin working part-time, usually after your 3rd year as an undergraduate. "With a pre-dental or biology major you can't get work right away in your field."

CAREER CHECKLIST

You'll like this job if you ...

Want to ease people's pain

Can get along with different personalities

Don't mind always working in one, small place

Will work long hours

Can work under time limits

Like science

Are organized

Variety is the Spice of Life

After graduating from college, Kim got a job working for a dentist in St. Petersburg. She was working 4 days a week, making good money, and enjoying life. As time went on, she began to want more variety in her work. She watched the dentist and thought, " I could do that; in fact, I bet I could do it better." It was an easy decision to go from hygiene to dentistry, she says, and she began to prepare herself. To be qualified for dental school, she took a year's worth of part-time classes in heavy sciences like biochemistry and physics. She had taken the required trigonometry and calculus in high school.

Kim applied for dental school, but she also applied to work in Switzerland on a year's contract. Because of

We're constantly taking courses,
learning new things.
I enjoy doing crown and
bridge work,
which restores teeth and
sometimes replaces
missing teeth
so patients can function better.

a labor shortage, the Swiss government was offering jobs to U.S. hygienists 26 years old or younger. Before Kim heard from Switzerland, she was accepted into dental school at Loyola University in Chicago.

Although her parents helped her, Kim had to take out loans and seek scholarship money to attend dental

want to help women get a higher education. The DAR (Daughters of the American Revolution) actually gave me money, not a loan."

"As a dental hygienist, I had learned how to work in people's mouths and organize my time. This made the clinical sessions in dental school very easy for me. It also al-

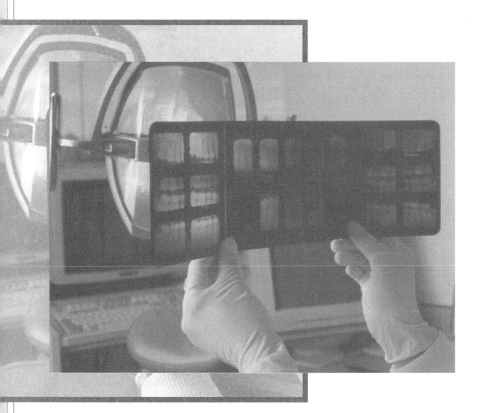

school. "I approached every organization I could think of," she says. "There are groups out there that

lowed me time to work." During her senior year Kim was able to work part-time as a hygienist, earning

$20,000 toward her schooling. When Kim graduated at age 30, she owed about $65,000. "The average dental cial studies. She took a job in an office near Baltimore. "I took the job because I liked the partners and

> # Most people hate coming to the dentist because there is always fear involved. You have to be able to use psychology with some patients.

school tuition is about $12,000 a year; then there are the tools you need, books, and living expenses."

From Associate to Owner

Kim worked as an associate in a dentist's office when she returned to St. Petersburg. She decided to move to Maryland, because a friend, who was also a dentist, had been accepted into the University of Maryland for spe-

thought they'd be good employers. It was good experience. I worked in a clinic atmosphere where we performed all aspects of dentistry, which included root canals, fillings, oral surgery, gum work, and so forth."

Then she met her future husband, Jay. "He was a cousin of my boss, and he came there for his dental work. We dated for a year and then got married." When they married, they lived in Virginia, so Kim had to take the regional board exams to get her license to practice in Virginia.

"I'm so glad I married Jay. I love having him in a different industry (Personal Communication Industry Association). He deals with totally different issues and people."

In Virginia, Kim worked as an associate for about 2 years before she bought a practice. "I started working for a dentist on a 6-month trial basis so we could get to know each other. I was surprised when he asked me if I was interested in buying his practice. He was only 54 years old. He had been in the same office for 25 years so he had a good client base and our dental philosophy was the same."

Within a year, Kim managed to buy the practice. She had observed how the office ran and seen the financial reports. The retiring dentist financed some of the money and Kim got a bank loan, but because she was married, the bank insisted her husband sign on the loan so he was also obligated to

pay the money. A few years later, when Kim moved into new offices with new equipment, she was able to get a loan under her signature alone.

"I enjoy the business part of dentistry as much as the clinical," says Kim "In dental school you are not taught how to run a small business. I have an annual budget and monthly financial statements to keep me on

business, has been a wonderful asset to me over the years."

Those 3-day Weekends

While Kim works long hours, she believes in a balanced life of work and leisure. She is always attending study clubs or taking classes, because continuing education is a big part of dentistry. Kim exercises every night with

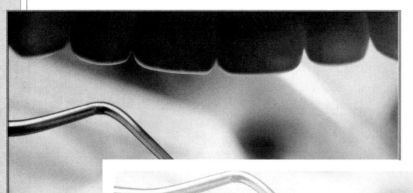

top of things. It cost me $250,000 to build my new office, a debt I have to pay off in 5 years. My husband, who has a lot of experience in running a

equipment she has in her basement. She loves gardening and sports like golfing, biking, snow skiing, and scuba diving. "When we go skiing, ten of us rent a house, usually out West." Sometimes Jay's work requires travel and Kim can close the office and go with him. "One of our best trips was to Hong Kong and Singapore."

Kim loves her practice and plans no big changes. She thinks eventu-ally she will hire an associate or get a partner, so when she takes a trip the business can stay open to serve her patients. When she retires, she hopes she can sell her business to a woman dentist.

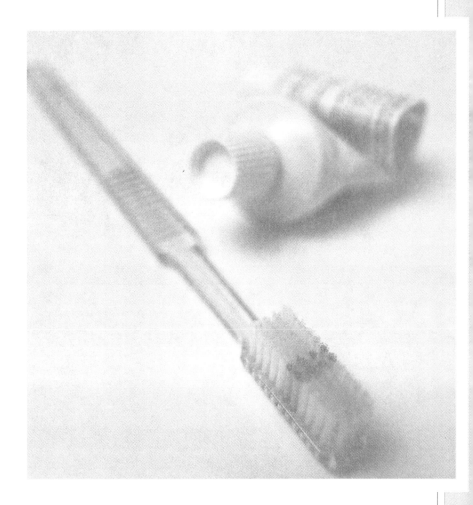

Barbara S. Silbert

Barbara S. Silbert

Barbara S. Silbert, D.C., N.C., Private Practice, Brookline and Newburyport, MA

Major in Sociology; master's degree in Gerontology; D.C., Western States Chiropractic School Portland, OR; N.D., Bastyr University of Natural Health Sciences, Seattle, WA

Chiropractic & Naturopathic Physician

She Treats the Whole Person

Dr. Barbara Silbert never knows what type of patients she will see from one day to the next. In a single day, she will see patients with a number of different illnesses or complaints. For example, she might see a patient who needs to be treated for depression, one with an ear or sinus infection, a woman who is trying to get pregnant, and someone with a serious disease such as cancer or Alzheimer's. As a naturopathic physician, Barbara looks at the whole person, tries to find causes of illness, and uses natural methods to treat her patients. She will consider the patient's mental, emotional, and physical health and offer treatment that helps the patient stay healthy over time.

CHIROPRACTIC DOCTOR, NATUROPATHIC DOCTOR

Experienced in private practice, $40,000 to $150,000

High school
honor
student

Creates women's
studies program,
graduates UCLA

Gets
master's
in gerontology

Naturopathic physicians are one of the best-kept secrets in the world, Barbara says. They are the experts who are educated, trained, and tested in natural medicine. There are between 1,200 and 1,500 trained and educated naturopaths practicing in the United States today. Barbara uses herbs, homeopathy (the principle of like-cures-like, in very small doses), nutrition counseling, lifestyle counseling, and chiropractic services to ease pain, cure illness and disease, and help the patient improve overall health.

"My personal bent is that I don't like to prescribe too many meds. I'd rather do what I can with helping a patient change their lifestyle. We always look at the whole person, rather than just treating a patient's symptoms. I have to know everything a conventional medical doctor would know and all about botanical (herbal) medicine (Barbara treats the patients with western herbs), homeopathy, nutrition, and chiropractic care as well." (Only 16.5% of chiropractors are women.)

She Listens

When she sees a new patient, Barbara will spend at least an hour and one half talking to the patient about health and any recent problems the patient has had. Some people come to Barbara for chiropractic care after an injury. Many people come to see Barbara because they are interested in staying healthy and preventing disease. Others come because they have tried everything else and are

desperate for help with a serious illness. Barbara never attempts to treat an acute illness on the first visit. She has to get to know more about the person first so that she can prescribe a treatment that will address not just symptoms, but the patient's whole mental, emotional, and physical state.

"People say they couldn't possibly spend so much time talking about their health, but I usually have to push them out the door at the end of their time," Barbara says. "This is a time when I can think more deeply about who they are; about the big picture. People begin making connections when they relate their history. I'll say, when did you start feeling this way, and they may realize that this began when they suffered a trauma such as the divorce of their parents or some other event which changed their life and their health status."

"There is some uncertainty involved in what I do. I never know who is coming through the door and what problem they have. With conventional medicine, the patient almost always leaves with a prescription and doesn't usually question whether this is the best thing for the particular situation. But with naturopathic medicine, we try to find the causes and then treat the person, so it takes longer. I know that a patient will eventually get better; I'm not always sure how long that process will take."

Barbara has seen some big changes in patients who come to see her. For example, she has good results with patients who are being treated by conventional doctors for Alzheimer's.

59

BARBARA'S CAREER PATH

Opens own
▼ practice,
moves to
Massachusetts

Gives talks, writes,
▼ promotes profession

"Many times the patient is on so many medications that it is the medicines that are confusing them, not the disease," Barbara says.

Barbara believes she and other naturopaths provide the best health care possible and sometimes dramatically improve the health of their patients. Because she loves what she does and naturopathy is not yet well understood by most people, Barbara spends a lot of time explaining the naturopathic way of thinking to different types of people. She talks to legislators, who she hopes will pass laws so that the profession

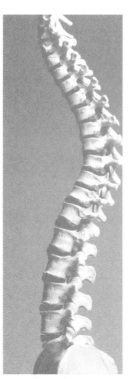

can be held to national standards like other medical doctors. She talks to educators, who can help people understand what to look for when selecting a naturopath, and potential patients, many of whom don't understand the difference between a naturopath and other types of doctors and health care providers. Barbara also writes columns for local newspapers and articles for national magazines, appears on television, and lobbies the state legislature to pass laws that will assure that people who call themselves naturopaths have the education and training pre-

60

scribed by the American Association of Naturopathic Physicians. She is President of the Massachusetts Society of Naturopathic Physicians.

The Middle Child

Barbara grew up in Hull, Massachusetts, a beautiful peninsula town that attracted hoards of summer vacationers and became a sleepy hamlet in the winter. She played a little basketball and was an honor student in school. She was a shy girl, the middle child between an older brother and two younger twin sisters.

Even though she was always good in school and knew that she was college bound, she had no idea that she would end up as a doctor. When it came time to go to college, she chose the University of California at Los Angeles. She had some relatives who had moved to Southern California and the idea of being far from home appealed to her. "I definitely needed to get out of town. Hull was such a small town that I left regularly to see

CAREER CHECKLIST

You'll like this job if you ...

- Like to analyze problems and solve puzzles
- Really want to care for people
- Believe that nutrition and lifestyle dramatically influence health
- Are willing to spend years educating yourself
- Have patience to find the causes of things
- Have an open mind

GROUNDBREAKERS

The First Textbook

Minora Paxson co-authored the first textbook for the profession of Chiropractic. Three of the first "15 disciples" of D.D. Palmer's Chiropractic School and Cure were women. By the 1920s, one third to one half of practicing chiropractors were women. There was a backlash after World War II, and the numbers of women chiropractors declined. Today only 16.5 percent are women.

Source: *The American Homeopath Journal* (1997) National Center for Homeopathy

---

other people. Because my mother's siblings had moved to Southern California when I was little, at least I had some safety out there. UCLA was overwhelming that first year. I had grown up in a seasonal town, 7,000 to 10,000 in the winter and double in the summer, and UCLA had 35,000 people on the campus. I had to park my car several miles away, with my bike in the trunk, and ride my bike from class to class because the campus was so big. It was very different!"

In college, Barbara studied sociology, philosophy, and women's studies. In fact, she helped to begin the first women's studies program at UCLA. "In those days they didn't have women's study courses, so some friends and I basically organized the women's studies program. I was the co-founder and co-mother of the women's studies student union. I wrote a newsletter and got courses together, and I was the first or second one to graduate with that specialization."

Barbara had some teachers in high school who made her think hard about the effects her actions would have on other people. "I was always a golden rulist, 'do unto others as you would have them do unto you.' I felt sociology and women's studies gave aging) from Goddard-Cambridge, Goddard's graduate program for social change. "The whole idea was that we were supposed to work in collectives and teach each other," Bar-

> In my first session with a patient, I'll say, when did this happen? Eventually, things fall together, light bulbs start going off, and they start to get an idea of why they are the way they are.

me the humanistic approach that I was looking for."

After she graduated from UCLA, Barbara went on to get a master's degree in gerontology (the study of bara says. "But when we got there people weren't really doing the collective thing. I had signed up for women and aging and no one else had. They ended up putting me with

I ask that all my patients have a primary physician other than me—an M.D.— in case they have any unfortunate catastrophe fall upon them. That way they can have hospitalization or conventional pharmaceuticals if they need them.

another group that was learning about health education and aging and social services with a feminist perspective, so I wrote my thesis in- dependently on women and aging. There weren't any gerontology pro- grams at the time. I got one of the first masters in gerontology."

ment of illness and disease by working on the joints of the human body. A series of auto accidents, preceded by having a woodpile fall on her and the death of her best friend, changed her life.

Understanding that a patient isn't working, or their car is broken, or the activities of daily living are being impacted by their physical state or mental or emotional state will influence my treatment. I try to help them understand how to take care of themselves.

A Fear of Dying

Barbara worked as a social worker with disabled and elderly adults for five years. She was the director of the adult foster care program for a city in Massachusetts. But fear of dying led her to study chiropractic, the treat-

"My best friend in the world died when I was 27. At around the same time, I was injured several times during a 4-month period. I could barely walk. Each time I tried to go back out I got injured again. I was at the chiropractor's office so often that I was bored. Waiting for him, I would

GROUNDBREAKERS

She Preserved the Practice of Homeopathy

Julia Minerva Green, one of 15 women in her class, graduated in 1898 from the Boston University School of Medicine. At that time it was still a homeopathic school. (Homeopathy was founded by Samuel Hahnemann who developed the principle "Let likes cure likes" into a system of medicine. He wrote the Organon and volumes of case notes.) Green practiced in Washington, DC and is said to have made house calls on a bicycle, having lead weights sewn into the hem of her skirt to keep it in place while she pedaled.

In 1922, with the closing of all the homeopathic schools, she realized that homeopathy might be lost. She gathered together a group of like-minded physicians and formed the American Foundation for Homeopathy (now the National Center for Homeopathy). The AFH offered a 6-week postgraduate course and was responsible for training the generation of homeopaths before and during World War II. Julia Green had a solid vision of what homeopathy was and how its business should be conducted. She died in 1963 at the age of 92.

Source: *The American Homeopath Journal* (1997)
National Center for Homeopathy

pull the books off the shelves and start reading them. Finally he said 'Barbara, my wife has the catalogues for chiropractic school, why don't you look at them?' That was in November. In January I was doing my prerequisites at Salem State University in Salem, Massachusetts, and decided I was going to chiropractic school in September."

Barbara chose Western States Chiropractic School in Portland, Oregon, after discussing with some chiropractors which were the best schools. There she studied chiropractic theory and practice, as well as other areas of medicine—radiology, gynecology, minor surgery, nutrition, and clinical laboratory work. "There are two types of schools for chiropractors," she says, "the pure and the mixer schools. In the pure schools, everything is related to treatment of the joints. In the mixer schools, they believe that you should also know about other areas of medicine."

In her third year Barbara discovered a naturopathic medical school just a couple of miles away from

Western State, and she took some classes there on top of what she was taking at Western State. "That's when I realized why I was on this planet. I knew naturopathic medicine was something I needed to do."

After she had her chiropractic degree, she entered Bastyr University of Natural Health Sciences in Seattle with an advanced standing, because of the work she had done while in chiropractic school. It is one of four schools in the United States that grants an N.D. (Doctor of Naturopathy) degree that is accredited by the U.S. Department of Education. She had to serve an internship, or preceptorship, with a doctor in Seattle, and she studied for 10 days at a clinic in Mexico that treats seriously ill patients. Because there is so much to learn in her field, she still studies all the time. She currently is taking a 3-year course from an Indian physician in what is now her home state of Massachusetts. She has studied with experts in botanical medicine, homeopathy, and nutrition in New York City and London.

Barbara's first work as a naturopath and chiropractor was in Seattle, where she shared an office with another chiropractor. After less than a year, she opened her own practice, and shared her practice with an acupuncturist and a massage therapist. The decision to practice in the East was driven by a desire to return to where some long-time friends lived and to the roots of her family. She has now been in practice 10 years. She has recently opened a practice in Brookline, Massachusetts, just outside of Boston, three days a week, and practices in Newbury, Massachusetts, one day a week. On her days off, she has time to exercise, to reflect on her patients, to write articles and columns, and to see friends.

garlic

Nadine Eads

Nadine Eads, FNP, Community Outreach Director, Washington Hospital Center, Washington Cancer Institute, DC

Major in Nursing Science, master's degree in Nursing Science

Family Nurse Practitioner

The Voice of the Patient

Nadine Eads' first job as a newly graduated nurse practitioner was as coordinator of a new project at Washington Hospital Center. Her job: to screen women in the African American community of Washington, DC, for breast and cervical cancer at no charge to the women.

"They wanted someone to coordinate and run the project but also someone qualified to do the initial examinations," says Nadine. A nurse practitioner—a registered nurse with advanced academic and clinical experience—can do many things a physician can do, including examine, diagnose, and prescribe medications and treatments.

Nadine's job was to perform a screening physical, which included examination of the breast and cervix,

LICENSED PRACTICAL NURSE

- Average $18,000 to $26,500

Source: *Career Information Center* (6th ed.). (1996). New York: Simon & Schuster.

REGISTERED NURSE

- Average Beginning $27,000
- Range $22,000 to $75,000

Source: *Encyclopedia of Careers and Vocational Guidance.* (1997). Chicago: J. G. Ferguson

NURSE PRACTITIONER

- Range from $40,000 to $100,000

PHYSICIAN'S ASSISTANT

- Range from $30,000 to $100,000

Source: *Encyclopedia of Careers and Vocational Guidance.* (1997). Chicago: J. G. Ferguson

Ill as child, admires nurses

Top student, cheerleader, French club, track

At Howard U a leader, sorority, ROTC

explain the importance of and process for doing a self-exam of the breasts, schedule mammograms, review radiology and laboratory results, and help with follow-up treatment if indicated. If the women

was asked to coordinate the Breast Care Center.

"I was performing breast exams every day, which increased my abil-

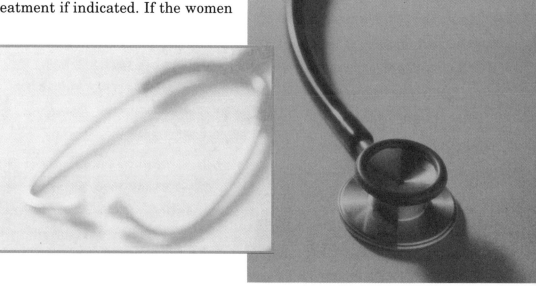

were diagnosed with breast cancer, Nadine arranged for a team of cancer experts to evaluate the patient and recommend treatment options. As a result of her work on this project, she

ity to find cysts or lumps. I would consult with physicians by telephone before or after patient visits to discuss the breast examinations. Also

Graduates RN,
▼ works in hospital

Specializes in
▼ labor & delivery

Graduates family
▼ nurse practitioner

the senior residents (students completing their education) came to the center to observe breast examination techniques. The key to fighting cancer is detecting it in its early stages."

This project gave Nadine lots of visibility in Washington, DC. She became the "breast guru," and was invited to speak on radio and television about breast cancer outreach activities and how important it is for all women to perform self-exams and learn about breast cancer symptoms.

Because of the success of the project, the management at Washington Hospital Center decided to change Nadine's role to outreach—going out into the community to find partners who will help the hospital provide its services to more people. Nadine's previous role was taken over by others. She started writing grants and got funds to do a conference. She had the honor of being part of a breast cancer assessment team of volunteers for Project Hope (People-to-People

NADINE'S CAREER PATH

Joins breast
▼ cancer
project

Trip to Budapest for Project
▼ HOPE

Health Foundation programs that promote better health worldwide through training health personnel in developing countries) and traveled to Budapest.

"It is because of my role as a nurse practitioner and my interaction with patients that I'm now able to articulate, be the voice of the patient, who is the consumer of health services. I want to make sure the outreach program is of value to them." For example, Nadine came up with the idea for a program called First Ladies Club. Women in predominantly African American churches volunteer for 14 hours of free training to learn about breast cancer risk factors, screening methods, treatment options, and community resources. The women then serve as a resource for other church members. Nadine meets with them monthly. Their first event was Hats Off to Breast Health, a hat fashion show which also offered information about breast cancer. "This is an exam-

ple of how learning can be combined with fun and entertainment."

Though most of Nadine's work originally focused on breast cancer, she is now responsible for developing and implementing public education campaigns for other types of cancer and setting up public-private partnerships with business, church, and civic organizations. She coordinates special events like the National Race for the Cure for breast cancer. She was featured as a nurse expert in some of the hospital's television commercials. "TV is a powerful way to teach people where they are most comfortable, at home."

Meetings in the Morning

A typical day for Nadine starts about 7:30 a.m., usually with a meeting because her work involves people from other departments and community partners. "I have about six or seven projects I'm working on at one time. I manage by time lines—doing what

CAREER CHECKLIST ✔

You'll like this job if you ...

Genuinely care about the well being of others

Will study and keep learning

Can do public speaking, are persuasive, can convince others to help in worthy causes

Love being responsible, your own boss

Are highly organized

Will take care of your own health

GROUNDBREAKERS

Women Care for Civil War Wounded

Modern nursing began in the U.S. during the Civil War, 1860-1865, when the women's care of the wounded proved that attention to proper sanitation, cleanliness, nourishing diet, and comfort cut the death rate enormously.

These early nurses bartered 2 or 3 years of service to hospitals for a diploma which allowed them to practice independently. By the early 1920s, the American Nursing Association (ANA) was created, and it developed registration laws, which were voluntary. In the 1950s, registration became a legal prerequisite to practice.

Source: *The Reader's Companion to Women's History*. (1998). NY: Houghton Mifflin

has to be done in stages. I have an administrative assistant who helps me, and I often call from my car phone and ask her to do letters or set appointments."

Nadine has a natural talent for salesmanship. She is an advocate. "I feel as a nurse practitioner I'm selling the message 'this is what you can do for yourself.' I am selling life-saving messages like: 'you should check your breasts every month.' I sell private organizations the opportunity to partner with our hospital for various health promotion activities. I also sell creative health programs through grant writing proposals to obtain funding for outreach services."

The work day ends around 4 p.m. but Nadine rarely goes straight home. She may go to her health club and work out for an hour. She may have to catch a train or plane to attend a conference or meeting out of town. Though Nadine no longer provides direct clinical care, she frequently works as an "advice nurse" for the health care organization, Kaiser Permanente. She talks over

> "It's an honor to be a part of the great moments of life, like birth, and have the ability to help during the traumatic times of injury, illness, even death. Being able to give to others is so rewarding."

the telephone to members who call in with a range of health problems, from cold symptoms to chest pain. Because of Nadine's caring approach in handling calls, her advanced clinical skills, and being vocal about enhancing job performance, she was asked to help with training new advice nurses.

A Young Advocate

As a young girl, Nadine was shy and sickly. If there was a "bug" going around, she would catch it. She also was rather headstrong, like the time at her house she wanted more strawberry punch, but her mother, who was cleaning up after the party, said no. Two-year-old Nadine found some pink stuff and drank it anyway, but it turned out it was furniture polish! She developed a high fever and was rushed to the hospital. This hospital experience, and another when at nine she ate lots of cherries and found she was allergic, were memorable because of the nurses, who treated her so well.

"They were the ones who told me

when my mother was coming to visit, who held me when I cried, who played cards with me, who helped me get well. We lived near the hospital, and I would watch the nursing students from our window. My mother wanted to be a nurse, but never had the educational opportunity. She told me I'd be a wonderful nurse. I also thought about being an attorney when I was in college, but I had decided in fifth grade I'd be a nurse."

Nadine did well in school. She grew up in Buffalo, New York. There, in 1967, she first experienced integration in the fifth grade—from then on she went to predominantly white schools with a vigorous academic program. "I integrated the French Club, and I was the third African American to become a varsity cheerleader." Nadine planned to get her bachelor's degree in nursing sci-

ence, but she knew she'd need to have more than good grades, she'd need to have extra curricular activities. "I have a very dear friend, Corri, who is White. We were the dynamic duo. She influenced me most about what all the activities would mean to

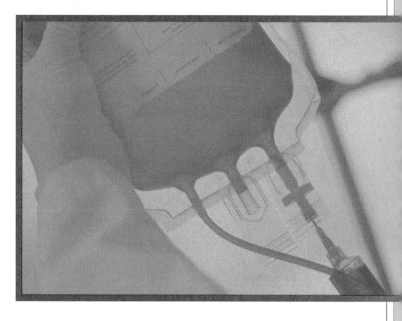

getting into a good college. I did sports, loved track, but I had to be sure I could get home by the city bus by early evening, because it was clear that African Americans had no business in that neighborhood after dark."

After graduation, often being the

only African American in a group, Nadine decided she needed to have a better understanding of who she was as an African American woman. She discovered Howard University in Washington, DC—a university that has graduated many African American leaders.

Nadine spent 5 years getting her bachelor's degree. The work was hard, but after a year or two she enjoyed it more and found time to join in campus activities, expressing her ideas, speaking out, taking leadership roles. She was in the army ROTC, the sorority Alpha Kappa Alpha, and was president of the nursing school student council for three years. In 1996, she was invited back to Howard to give a commencement speech.

A Specialty Decision

Nadine's first job as a registered nurse was in Howard University's infirmary, taking care of students. "I wanted a role that would allow me a social life. I had evenings and weekends off for a whole year." Nadine took care of ill students and dispensed medication. Her fellow nurses, who had hospital experience, inspired her to seek a job in a hospital. She took a job at George Washington Hospital, taking care of women patients in for surgery. Many were ill with cancer. "My first cancer patient was a 14-year-old girl going through chemotherapy."

After a year, Nadine felt that she needed a specialty, but "I wanted something fun." It was in the mid 1970s and a tremendous nursing shortage made it easy for Nadine to move to the labor and delivery unit at the hospital. "You come prepared with general knowledge, then you learn the special skills needed. For example, a nurse will have general skills to care for a diabetic, but if that woman is pregnant, it is much more complex."

Nadine's work was with high-risk patients. "I loved living on the edge. We could go from having no patients to an emergency life or death situation, like a pregnant woman injured in an auto accident." Nadine became assistant head nurse. "Working with pregnant women was the best choice for me. It gave me a higher understanding of other specialties like anesthesia, intensive care, neonatal, and maternal-fetal medicine. I had the opportunity to practice collabora-

needed to during the day, and I had every other weekend off. I was single, it worked for me."

A Wish To Do More

Nadine worked 10 years as a nurse before she started her two-year nurse practitioner studies at Howard

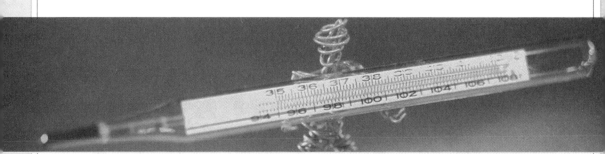

tively, seeing physicians as equal colleagues who appreciated my observations and assessments. Nurses are the patient's eyes, ears, everything."

Nadine worked nights, 11 p.m. to 7 a.m. "Because there were fewer routine procedures at night, and fewer backup staff, you were forced to learn everything. You were in charge. You got more opportunities to hone your skills. I felt I could do everything I

University. In that time she learned to take care of herself, but she admits she's a workaholic. Nadine has asthma and says, "My patients made me promise to take care of myself so I could continue to care for other patients." Nadine has also learned to balance career with pleasure. "I have a high level of commitment to my work, and I work hard, but I also play." Nadine enjoys traveling (especially to Cancun, Mexico), reading, and getting together with friends.

As to the future, Nadine wants to use her clinical expertise in public policy work. "There are many policy makers who have zero or limited clinical experience. I would like use my experience to shape policy, so health care is really valuable to all people, so it is accessible and available to babies, children, youth, and adults."

Amy Nathans

Amy Nathans

Amy Nathans, CNM, The Physician and Midwife Collaborative Practice, Alexandria, VA

Major in Nursing Science, master's degree in Public Health, master's degree in Science of Nursing

Certified Nurse
Midwife

The Birth Expert

The door to Amy Nathans' office is a bulletin board with photos of happy newborn babies and their proud parents. Amy is a certified nurse midwife (CNM). She works in an office in Alexandria, Virginia, that includes two doctors and six midwives. But she could work on her own or on a hospital staff; and she could deliver babies in the home, in a hospital, or in a birth center.

Amy is a registered nurse from a 4-year college program and has extra training she received in graduate school. CNMs are certified and licensed to care for women who are experiencing a normal pregnancy and birth (at low risk to have any trouble). They care for the woman before the birth, they help during the birth, they deliver the baby, and they care

NURSE MIDWIFE

Starting salary $31,000

Average earnings $45,000 to $71,000

for the woman afterward. However, in the United States, midwives must have a physician on call and available when they are delivering the babies, just in case a doctor is needed for the mother or the baby. Midwives cannot do any surgery, although they can perform some minor surgical tasks like stitches.

"We see birth as a normal process that women go through, not some illness. We trust in women's bodies to have babies, so we don't automatically use lots of technology. As a matter of routine, we're low-tech," says Amy.

Amy had her two babies at home. "It was wonderful to walk around my house, go into the kitchen and get a drink from my own glass, and get in my own shower, my own bathtub."

Amy's patients go a hospital to have their babies, but the midwives help make the experience like a home birth. "Making the woman move is one of the things in our 'bag of tricks' to make birth more comfortable." Amy encourages the woman to walk around, squat, rock, get on hands and knees—all designed to let gravity help with the birth. Taking a soothing bath, munching an apple, and drinking juice help the woman relax. Amy monitors what is going on with the baby at all times.

"We want what the woman wants. If she wants a pain killer, we will give what is called an epidural anesthesia. The shot is delivered between the lower vertebrae in the spine and the anesthesia numbs from the waist down. But many woman have babies without any pain medication."

Transfers to DC
▼ college, graduates as registered nurse

Works trauma center, then
▼ health administration

Studies midwifery,
▼ marries Joe

A Full Day

Amy's day starts early when she gets her two boys—4-year-old Sam and 8-month-old Zev—and herself ready for childcare. "If we have a third child, we're thinking of Joe staying home with the children." Joe works for a company that moves the materials used during large conventions and meetings. But Amy is the family's top

> We see birth as a normal process that women go through, not some illness. We trust in women's bodies to have babies, so we don't automatically use lots of technology.

the day. Amy's husband, Joe Fishman, helps a great deal with the child rearing, yet Amy still spends more than $1,000 per month for wage earner. "We're both in the delivery business," she says.

The drive to the office takes Amy 45 minutes each way. She enjoys the

Has two
children

Leaves hospital to
join private practice
group

rare peace and quiet of being alone. She arrives at work around 8 a.m. and will see a mix of patients. One patient is there for a well-woman annual checkup. A pregnant woman is

getting checked at the first of her scheduled 14 visits—the first visit is 30 minutes, all the rest are 15 minutes long. Another has a problem; and another is in for tests. Besides seeing patients, Amy answers phone calls, looks at test results, consults with fellow midwives and the doctors, and calls patients. Sometimes she speaks before groups about pregnancy and midwifery.

"What I like best about the work is the interaction with the women. The most pleasurable part is counseling, having time to talk to people and listen to their concerns, their fears, and help them understand what's happening. Many

women are educated and know what they want. They ask lots of questions, and we get them the answers if we don't know. Other women may not know they want a midwife until they meet us; then they love us. We have more time than doctors to ask such things as: How's the exercise coming? Did you have time to get your feet up? What are you eating?"

When Amy is on call, she may spend 24 hours at the hospital without sleep and have to catch up the next day. "More babies are born at night," she says. "I love the excitement and urgency. I get an adrenaline rush being there, catching the babies as they come into the world."

Amy has attended more than 450 births, more than many midwives who, like her, have been out of school only 5 years. That's because her first job as a midwife was with a public hospital that cared for poor women and many immigrant women who didn't speak English. Midwives there saw about 40 patients a day and a visit was 5 or 10 minutes long. "I learned to speak Spanish, though not

CAREER CHECKLIST ✓

You'll like this job if you ...

- Can deal with "blood and guts"

- Can do without sleep at times

- Like to help women and babies

- Can be calm in stressful situations

- Can work with all types of people

- Believe the human body is a great creation

GROUNDBREAKERS

The Oldest Profession

Care of women during childbirth is probably the oldest of women's professions. In the United States, childbirth moved from midwives to doctors in the middle of the 19th Century and from homes to hospitals in the early 20th Century.

Source: *The Reader's Companion to Women's History.* (1998). NY: Houghton Mifflin

real well. I could say 'El niño viene. Yo veo el pelo de la cabeza.' (The baby is coming, I can see the hair.) The women forgave my poor accent."

Amy worked there almost 5 years. "I learned so much. We had so many patients that you tend to see everything at least once. I've seen all kinds of unusual births that others have just read about."

When Amy was on maternity leave with her second baby, she thought a lot about her job. First, she realized she was seeing so many patients a day that she was working on "auto pilot." She wasn't really interacting with the women and getting to know them. Second, she realized there was a huge difference between how she had her babies at home and how she was delivering babies at the hospital with what she calls "techno birth." Third, the hospital was increasing its demands on the salaried midwives to see more patients and spend more hours working and visiting clinics.

"Several of us midwives met with management and said how unhappy we were about the demands on us.

Always knew I'd be in a health profession, helping others, but I didn't know what I'd do. I was fascinated with the human body and never felt grossed out when someone was cut and bleeding. I was more in awe

We were told that was how it was and if we didn't like it we could find a new job. So I did. I actually took a pay cut, but now I'm helping women have more natural, 'low tech' births. I'm getting to really know the women as individuals. I love it."

High School Was a Drag

Amy grew up in Bellport, New York, the youngest of five children. Her father was a physicist. Her mother was a homemaker when the children were small, but now is an artist who also weaves and does bead work. "I

GROUNDBREAKERS

Frontier Nursing

In 1925, Myra Breckenridge (1881-1965) founded a service that sent nurses and midwives to remote areas of Kentucky, lowering the infant and maternal death rate. It became Frontier Nursing Service in 1928 when she also founded the Frontier Graduate School of Midwifery. In 1929, she cofounded the American Association of Nurse Midwives. Her autobiographical book, written in 1952, is *Wide Neighborhoods: Story of Frontier Nursing Service.*

Source: Irene M. Franck & David M. Bromstone. (1995). *Women's World.* NY: HarperCollins

always knew I'd be in a health profession, helping others, but I didn't know what I'd do. I was fascinated with the human body and never felt grossed out when someone was cut and bleeding. I was more in awe."

Amy hated high school. "It was a drag. I was too smart and it bored me, but I didn't do real well. I never learned to study and did terrible on multiple choice tests. I was a geek, I didn't date, I hung with the smart kids." Amy had enough credits to graduate after her junior year, so her parents arranged for her to spend the next year in Israel at a kibbutz, which is a communal farm where all the members live together and share the work.

"My parents knew I was bored and wanted me to see a world where life is completely different from what I knew. When you live in a kibbutz, people are sharing a dining room, raising each others' kids, working in the fields together—it is a socialistic society. There all the kids go into the military when they are 17 years old, and they don't come out until they are 20. It was eye-opening to live in a country where guns are common, war is common. For example, 17-year-

she wasn't doing well, and she decided not to take a pre-med course. Instead, she left Drew and went to a

The most pleasurable part is counseling, having time to talk to people and listen to their concerns, their fears, and help them understand what's happening.

olds were talking about politics. Kids in my country didn't know anything about politics. It was life altering for me. I also had my first serious relationship there."

When Amy returned to the United States, she entered Drew University. She thought she'd be a doctor. But

community college to get the courses she needed to enter nursing school. She transferred to American University in Washington, DC, and in 1985 graduated as a registered nurse.

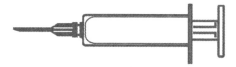

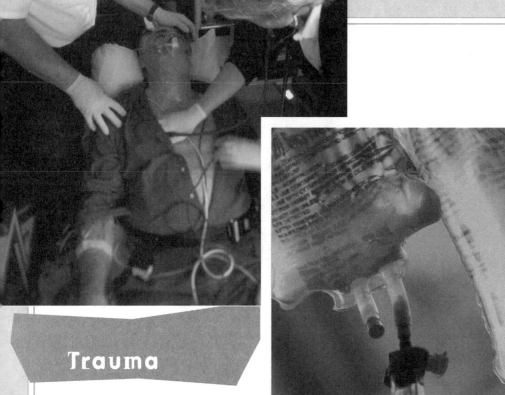

Trauma

Amy's first job as a nurse was in a trauma center in Baltimore, Maryland. She loved the fast pace, adrenaline rush, and the "blood and guts" work. She met her first husband there and moved to Washington, DC when they married. She then worked for a mini-emergency room, but decided she didn't want to be a nurse anymore and take orders from a doctor. She went back to school for one year and got a master's degree in Public Health. Then she took an administrative job with a large health organization. After about 3 years of administrative work, she realized she missed the clinical work with patients.

"About this time my marriage fell apart, and I was devastated. I thought about going back to nursing. The person who helped me most was a nun and midwife, Sister Hinnegan, who paved the way for me to become a midwife. With her help I applied for and received a grant to study midwifery at the University of Pennsylvania. My father agreed to pay the rest of the tuition.

"It was 18 months of a wonderful experience. It was adult learning. For the first time I was learning what I wanted to learn, not doing it because people made me. It was a combination of classroom then clinical, so I'd study, then get hands-on experience."

While she was a student, Amy met her current husband Joe at a community meeting. "We fell in love, and I said 'if you want to be with me you'll have to move to Washington.' My friends are there and my social group is important to me. He agreed and we got a place in Silver Spring, Maryland, which is in the DC metropolitan area."

Amy and Joe spend their leisure time caring for and enjoying their children. "We want to spend time with our kids. We recently spent two days in New York City without them and we missed them." Amy also enjoys knitting and is currently making memory books with all the snapshots she's taken of her children. Next, maybe she'll do memory books for the office midwives—of all the children they've helped bring into the world.

Sharon Frishett

Sharon (Shari) Frishett

Sharon (Shari) Frishett, Psychiatric Social Worker and Exercise Specialist at Suburban Hospital's Center for Integrative Medicine, Bethesda, MD

Major in Political Science, master's degree in Social Work, Clinical Mental Health specialty

Personal Trainer
and Counselor

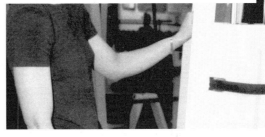

Her Tools Are Exercise and Nutrition

Sharon (Shari) Frishett is a personal trainer and counselor who specializes in body fat management. Shari, dressed in her sweats, is out the door by 5:30 most mornings and usually sees three clients at their homes before 10. She will spend an hour strength training (exercising with weights), showing them exercises and reviewing their progress. Today her first client is "Jeanne," a hard-driving, extremely successful businesswoman who used to weigh 310 pounds. When Jeanne's business partners and customers began telling her they were afraid to keep doing business with her because her weight made her so unhealthy she might not live much longer, Jeanne came to Shari for weight management counseling and exercise training. Jeanne

PERSONAL TRAINER

Salaries vary in this new area

SOCIAL WORKER/COUNSELOR

- Average earnings range from $20,000 to $60,000

Source: *Encyclopedia of Careers and Vocational Guidance.* (1997). Chicago: J. G. Ferguson

SHARI'S CAREER PATH

Graduates college, plays in rock band → Gets research job at Brookings Institute → Teaches aerobics

has lost more then 120 pounds with Shari's help.

Shari put Jeanne on an program of healthful, low-fat foods and cardiorespiratory exercises—fast walking and bike riding to burn body fat and strengthen her heart and lungs. Soon this routine became comfortable, and then Shari instructed Jeanne in the proper use of weights to build muscle mass and shape the body for optimal health. She also counsels Jeanne about nutrition. Shari goes to Jeanne's house for a training session three days a week. She spends most of her time weight training and teaching Jeanne flexibility (stretching) exercises to increase mobility and decrease risk of injury. Shari has helped Jeanne understand nutrition better and showed her how to take better care of herself through techniques such as meditation and yoga.

If you imagine your metabolism as a fire, the more muscle you have along with proper balanced nutrition, the hotter and steadier your fire will burn.

Gets certified as
sports trainer

Begins weight
management business

Works and
studies for
master's degree

Shari firmly believes proper nutrition and weight training are effective for losing fat, because building muscles increases the body's metabolism. Metabolism is the ability of the body to burn calories. "If you imagine your metabolism as a fire, the more muscle you have along with proper balanced nutrition, the hotter and steadier your fire will burn," Shari says. She also believes that for many people, admitting that you need to take good care of your body is important. Washington, DC, where Shari works, is a town where many smart people work very hard at thinking a lot. "These people are just walking, talking brains," Shari says. "They have dissociated themselves from their bodies. It's important to reconnect the mind with the body to stay healthy and fit."

Shari loves seeing the difference training with weights makes in peo-

ple, but she is also interested in more than just physical changes. She sees serious problems with weight, whether a person eats too much and becomes obese (overly fat), or a person's unhealthy eating patterns and preoccupations with body weight lead to an eating disorder like bulimia or anorexia. These are problems that need to be addressed through counseling with a professional. That's why Shari got a master's degree in Social Work (MSW) with a specialization in clinical mental health. With her MSW Shari has the professional tools to help people who have serious weight-related problems change their image of who they are and how they should live.

Part of the Job is Research

After her third client in the early morning hours, Shari heads for her office, where she changes into "office clothes," usually a nice business suit. Today her boss, Dr. Pamela Peeke, has asked her to do research into the healing effects of herbs for a lecture Dr. Peeke will give to 6,000 people later in the month. Shari uses the Internet to hook up to a database called Medline, which leads her to articles from scientific journals all over the world. Once she has gathered all the information in one place, Shari must read through it to see which studies are most credible and which she must discard. Shari knows that Dr. Peeke is counting on her to be accurate, and that the doctor will base her talk on the information Shari gathers, so it must be good! She will look at how many studies have been generated about a particular problem, whether the results have been repeated in other studies, and in which journals the articles are published. She will also get information about the authors of the studies, to decide if they may have a bias or slant in how they found the information. Finding authors who have credibility in the medical community is very important. She will find the most up-to-date, credible information and give it to Dr. Peeke for her talk. She will also prepare a bibliography for Dr. Peeke to hand out the audience.

After her search, Shari meets with a computer technician to discuss purchasing some new computers for the office. She and Dr. Peeke have set up a new clinic, the Suburban Hospital's Center for Integrative Medicine, in Bethesda, Maryland, just outside Washington, DC. The center will specialize in using integrative medicine to treat and prevent chronic and

CAREER CHECKLIST

This career is for you if you ...

Want to study the human body and how it moves

Like physical exercise

Are compassionate and want to help others

Can work long hours to achieve results

Can draw boundaries so you don't get overwhelmed by other people's problems

Believe in the power of the mind

GROUNDBREAKERS

Focus on Women's Health

In 1969 there was practically no women's health information easily available. A group of 12 young white feminists in Boston created the National Women's Health Network and published *Our Bodies, Ourselves*. It was an "underground" publication until 1973 when the first trade edition was published. Its frank presentation of women's health and sexuality helped encourage women to explore the health issues most important to them. The group, now called The Boston Women's Health Book Collective, has published other books. All book royalties go to women's health projects, especially its own Women's Health Information Center, Somerville, MA.

Source: *The Reader's Companion to Women's History.* (1998). NY: Houghton Mifflin.

lifestyle diseases such as cancer, heart disease, obesity, and eating disorders. Integrative medicine is a term defining an approach to health and wellness that combines conventional Western medicine with alternative therapies such as strength and flexibility training, acupuncture, nutrition therapy, hydrotherapy, meditation, and massage. Shari is excited about her role in helping to get the clinic off the ground. She will be doing training with weights and mental health counseling on weight-related issues with clinic patients.

Shari's next activity of the day is to sit in on a session with Dr. Peeke, her mentor and integrative medicine expert. Dr. Peeke was one of the founders of the National Institutes of Health Office of Alternative Medicine. Today, Dr. Peeke is seeing a famous man who has traveled across the country seeking help for his high blood pressure, obesity, and elevated cholesterol levels. He is unhappy and depressed and doesn't feel well, inside or out. Dr. Peeke believes the man is working too hard, and she tells him so. She counsels him to slow down and recommends that he spend more time with his family, as he is the proud father of a new baby girl. Shari quietly observes the doctor in her session with this patient. Later, Shari and Dr. Peeke will discuss the case together and use it as a learning tool for how to counsel patients. After many more sessions like this, Dr. Peeke eventually will allow Shari to see patients without supervision.

By this time it is about 6:00 in the evening. Shari is yearning for some exercise of her own, so she changes back into her sweats. She heads to a nearby

gym where she teaches a step aerobics class. After the class, Shari spends some time working out on her own with weight machines, then heads home to her apartment in Arlington, Virginia, just across the bridge from Washington. Shari goes to bed early.

Tomorrow will be another very full day. She must get up early to train one client, then she drives back to the office in Bethesda for the rest of the work day.

Shari works most Saturdays until two or three in the afternoon, although both she and Dr. Peeke will

dress casually, usually in exercise clothes and sneakers. Sunday she will teach another aerobics class, relax at home with friends, and Monday will begin another full week. Some nights Shari won't get home from work until 10:00 p.m.

From Weight Lifting to Weight Management

Shari discovered that she loved helping people learn to manage their weight and their lives effectively when she started teaching aerobics in 1989. Just after she  finished college, before she got into weight management counseling, she worked as a research assistant for a large Washington "think-tank," a research and political organization in Washington. The work was highly political and she didn't enjoy it much. "People were always tense, angry, and upset there," she says. "Of course that made them very nasty and unhappy, always trying to get what they wanted any way they could. Mentally, it was a very negative atmosphere and I found myself eating a lot more just because it seemed like it was the only 'fun' thing I did all day."

Because she was unhappy in her job, Shari spent lots of time doing what she loved—playing in a rock band she had formed with other musicians when she was in college and teaching aerobics classes at a local gym. She got her first job teaching aerobics by "just showing up and saying I wanted to do it!" After she tried out for the owners of the gym, they said, "Your music needs work but we like your style." They hired her to teach some classes. At that same time, she was spending a lot of time on her own in the gym lifting weights. Soon people started asking her about how to weight lift as if she were an expert. Shari started helping people informally, then realized that she enjoyed it so much that she might like to do it full-time for a living. "When I told my boss at the research center she laughed at me," Shari remembers. "She told me I would never make any money and I would be looking for my old job back within a year."

Shari studied and passed the Amer-

Try meditation, relaxation, or martial arts. These are great ways to make the mind/body connection— and relax, let go, and breathe!

ican Council on Exercise personal trainer certification exam in 1992. Next, Shari went to an office supply store and bought some computer software that helped her develop and write a business plan. She carefully put together a business plan for a weight management program combining healthy eating and lifestyle counseling with cardiovascular exercises, and training with weights to build muscle and increase metabolism. She took her plan to the leading health club in the Washington area and told them she wanted to start a weight management program for them. The health club agreed to hire her, not as an employee, but as an in-

dependent contractor. That meant that she was in business for herself, so she did not get health insurance or sick leave. If she didn't work, she did not earn any money. She also had to buy her own liability insurance.

She puts the emotion with the motion

Because she was so interested in helping people and was good at listening to what they had to say about struggling with weight and their physical and emotional problems, the customers liked Shari. She built

up a large list of satisfied clients, but she was struggling to make ends meet. The health club took a percentage of what she made per hour. Shari had almost enough money to pay her bills every month—her career in weight management had begun. She loved it, but also began to realize that she didn't truly have the right professional tools to help people deal with the complicated emotional part of losing weight and making lifestyle changes. Shari decided the MSW program at University of Maryland would give her these tools. By increasing her range of services, she could serve her clients better and make a better living for herself.

Shari attended a full schedule of classes and continued her work at the gym. She began to see that many body weight problems are caused by depression and anxiety, and the inability of hard-driving people to slow down and take better care of themselves. In her MSW classes, she learned all about therapeutic counseling. She got experience at a hospital working as an intern in the psychiatric and orthopedic wards.

She also worked as a counselor at a woman's center counseling women on just about any problem they wanted to talk about.

During this time, Shari kept hearing about Dr. Pamela Peeke, who was working at the National Institutes of Health on lifestyle diseases and integrative medicine. Shari told everyone she knew that she had to meet this doctor. Dr. Peeke also heard about Shari from some of her own patients who were using Shari to help them train with weights and exercise properly. It seemed like destiny that the women would finally work together. They are both interested in integrative medicine and in building strength in women as a counterbalance to the stress of modern living. Dr. Peeke started referring patients to Shari for training with weights, then hired Shari to work exclusively with her as she works with Suburban Hospital to build the Center for Integrative Medicine.

"Meeting Dr. Peeke changed my life," Shari says, "Here was a woman who was successfully doing everything I dreamed of in nutrition and lifestyle counseling, and she is also a marathon runner!" Dr. Peeke became an important mentor for Shari and helped guide her through the process of becoming accepted in the professional world. She also helped Shari make important decisions about how to focus her research and training in the last year of graduate school.

Dr. Peeke paid for Shari to get certified by the American College of Sports Medicine, the most prestigious (and academically difficult) of all of the fitness trainer certification exams. "Dr. Peeke also gave me another valuable gift—she showed me she believes in me by trusting me with enormous responsibility, giving me projects I would never dream I could do." At last, Shari is making a good salary and has good benefits like vacation and sick leave, health and dental insurance. She celebrated by buying her first new car.

Trailblazer

Shari hopes to do more research on weight management issues and to work more with eating disorders like bulimia and anorexia. "These are terrible illnesses," she says, "they are very hard to give up for people who have not developed other ways to deal with stress. Some people view their eating disorders as best friends! They keep them thin and relieve anxiety. Unfortunately, they can also permanently damage their health and even kill them."

Little has been written about the power of mental health counseling combined with exercise training and proper nutrition, and Shari thinks she will be able to blaze a trail in this field. She likes to be one of the first people to do something; and it's always been in her nature to blaze trails.

When she was a girl, Shari loved rock music and keeping fit through playing sports like soccer. In college she majored in political science and Russian studies, largely as a tribute to her father who has a Ph.D. and works in this field. "Dad and I used to talk about preventing nuclear war at the dinner table," she says. College taught her how to think critically and helped her get her first jobs in research, but it is the master's degree program that gave her the tools she needs to do the work she really loves.

Shari hasn't had much free time for a number of years now, but makes herself keep up with her friends so work doesn't overwhelm her life. "I really try to practice what I preach," she laughs. Shari talks to her best girlfriend daily and goes out with other friends at least once a week, usually on the weekends. She uses email a lot to keep in touch with friends and to make weekend plans. She recently returned from trip to Durango, Colorado, to visit with friends and take part in a 30-mile mountain bike marathon through the Colorado Rockies.

Shari, who is 31, is still single. "Eventually, I know I'll settle down with the right guy," she says, "but my schedule has been too busy for a serious relationship since I started graduate school. Maybe this coming year, who knows? Now I'm having a BLAST every day doing a job I love that makes a difference!"

More People Using Alternative Medicine

	1990	1997
Patients visits to practitioners of alternative therapies	427,120,000	628,825,000
Patients visits to all primary care physicians	387,558,000	385,919,000

Data are from *National Ambulatory Medical Care Survey from 1996 and 1990*, Hyattsville, MD: National Center for Health Statistics

Nanci Burchell

Nanci Burchell

Nancy Burchell, CNMT, The Children's Mercy Hospital, Kansas City, MO

Major in Biology and Chemistry, minor in Psychology

Nuclear Medical
Technologist

Nuclear Nanci

Nanci Burchell is the certified nuclear medical technologist for The Children's Mercy Hospital in Kansas City, Missouri. Nanci helps children by performing tests that show how parts of the body are working. She uses tracers—tiny amounts of radioactive compounds—that show up when filmed. Patients are injected with the tracers and a camera turns the light signals emitted by the tracers into electrical signals. The electrical signals are then turned into the images that are recorded on a film. The film is stored in a computer. Nanci has to prepare the images so they can be read by a radiologist, who will recommend treatment for the patient based on what the test shows.

"When a patient gets an X-ray or

NUCLEAR MEDICINE TECHNOLOGIST

Average $26,000 to $40,000

Source: *Encyclopedia of Careers and Vocational Guidance.* (1997). Chicago: J. G. Ferguson.

NANCI'S CAREER PATH

Summers with
▼ grandmother

Candy striper,
▼ first class
Girl Scout

Works in
▼ oncologist's
office

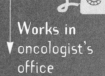

an ultrasound, the test usually deduces the size, shape, and other physical characteristics of an organ

performs over time. For example, I might perform a test to see if a child's kidney is obstructed or blocked. I

I'm not much taller than most kids.
I'm only five feet tall.
When I talk to the kids I try to
get to their level,
look them in the eyes.

or part of the body. But when you perform a nuclear medicine test, you are looking at how the organ or body part

would take pictures to observe how the tracer medicine makes its way through the kidney and how much

time it takes to get through. If it takes a long time, it might mean the kidney is obstructed," Nanci says.

The signals recorded on film produce an image showing the size and shape of the kidney and how it is working. The camera itself gives off

no radiation. In nuclear medicine, it is the patient who gives off the radiation. But no matter how many images are taken, the patient receives only one exposure dose—about the same amount of radiation as a chest X-ray.

Part of Nanci's job is to explain to the children she tests how the procedure works, so that they aren't frightened. She does this with all children who are old enough to understand. The tests help doctors determine what medical procedures are needed. For example, after looking at the results of a test, the doctor might say that a child will need surgery to correct a birth defect.

Nanci also explains the test procedure to the children's parents, because most people don't understand exactly what nuclear medicine is. "I often use the example of the phosphate compound, a chemical compound that latches on to the bones so we can take pictures of them. When you drink milk, you get phosphorus, which is good for your bones. The phosphate compound is another type of phosphorus."

After Nanci explains the procedure to the child and the parent, she pre-

NANCI'S CAREER PATH

Gets first job in Kansas City

Opens nuclear medicine program at Children's Mercy Hospital

pares and administers the radioactive chemical compounds, takes the pictures, and prepares the film to be read by the radiologist. Sometimes she also will give the patient a nonradioactive drug that helps with the tests.

To be a nuclear medicine technologist, you have to know about anatomy and physiology, radiation biology, radiation chemical compounds and other drugs, radiation safety, how to program and read the computer, and how to work with people well. Besides working with the children and their parents, Nanci works with five different radiologists at the hospital. The radiologist has to read the nuclear medicine test within 24 hours and get a report to the patient's doctor. This is especially important in cases where the doctor

will have to act quickly, such as when a bone is infected or a kidney is obstructed. Nanci also works with nurses, who sometimes will help get the patient ready for the tests. And Nanci works with other doctors to do research on how various treatments affect the body. She just completed her part of a study on how certain chemotherapy drugs affect the heart function over a long period of time.

A Busy Day

In a typical day, Nanci will see between five and seven patients. The hospital gets a lot of foreign-born parents and their children, and sometimes Nanci has to speak in French or Spanish to help people understand what's involved in the tests.

She schedules her own tests, so she spends part of her time on the phone with patients' parents or doctors. Some tests need to be done in stages—for example pictures will be taken every 2 hours over several hours to watch how things are working.

Nanci has an assistant who helps her when she is too busy to do everything herself or when she needs to be away from the nuclear medicine area. (Her assistant is from Chile and speaks five languages.) Part of Nanci's job is to educate the hospital staff about how to work safely with radiation, so sometimes Nanci goes to a different floor of the hospital to give a lecture or demonstration. She also travels to other cities to talk about nuclear medicine. She explains to other nuclear medicine technologists how to work with children, and she explains things about nuclear medicine to interested doctors who aren't radiologists or nuclear medicine physicians.

One of the best things about Nanci's job is that she gets to work with kids. "Everyone has their

CAREER CHECKLIST

You'll like this job if you ...

Love to work with children

Have a good sense of humor

Have a good grasp of math and science

Have good computer skills

Can work independently

Can explain things well

GROUNDBREAKERS

Nobel Prize Winner

Born in New York's South Bronx of Jewish immigrant parents, nuclear physicist Rosalyn Sussman Yalow (1921-) is codeveloper, with internist Solomon Berson, of RIA (radioimmunoassay) in 1950. RIA is a method of using radioactive particles to trace and measure minute amounts of substances such as hormones, enzymes, and drugs in blood and body tissue. It is an important tool in diagnosis. In 1977, she became the second woman to win a Nobel Prize for medicine.

She became chairman in 1968 of the department of medicine at New York Mount Sinai School of Medicine. She is the first woman to win the Albert Lasker Basic Medical Research Award, and in 1986 received the Georg Charles de Henesy Nuclear Medicine Pioneer Award.

Source: *The Reader's Companion to Women's History.* (1998). NY: Houghton Mifflin

niche," Nanci says. "Some people like working with elderly patients, but I much prefer pediatrics. Maybe that's because I'm not much taller than most kids. I'm only five feet tall. When I talk to the kids I try to get to their level, look them in the eyes. When people come for these tests, they are not themselves. Most of them are scared. You have to take that into consideration and explain things so people can understand. There is no excuse for using big words just to sound important."

Nanci tells the kids her name is Nuclear Nanci. It's a way for them to remember her, and it's a way to make the tests not quite so serious or scary. "We did a research study on kids who had cancer. Those who had been in remission for seven to ten years came back to see us. Some had even gotten married. They remembered me!"

One of Nanci's favorite things is holding babies. Because she works with lots of sick children, including children who have cancer, she likes to remember that her work often helps the kids get well. Holding the

When you perform a nuclear medicine test, you are looking at how the organ or body part performs over time. For example, I might perform a test to see if a child's kidney is obstructed or blocked.

babies makes her feel good. It helps her remember what's important about what she does.

Volunteered in Hospitals

When Nanci was a young girl, her younger brother was very sick with a tumor on his brain. They weren't sure if he would live. So Nanci, who grew up in Cape Girardeau, Missouri, spent summers with her grandmother in upstate New York while her mother took her brother to doctors. Today her brother is 38 years old. "It was sort of a miracle," Nanci says. She also has a sister who is two years younger. "My sister got all the artistic talent." she says.

Nanci was an active Girl Scout. To get to the level of first class scout, she volunteered as a candy striper in a hospital from the time she was 12 until she was 14. She learned a lot about how hospitals worked. When she was 16, her first job was for an oncologist (cancer doctor). Her job was to assess where the patients were emotionally—whether they had accepted the fact that they had cancer and how they were coping with that knowledge. The nuclear medi-

There is so much to learn. The changes in computer technology are changing the way nuclear medicine is practiced.

cine department was next door, and Nanci noticed that nuclear medicine was a profession where you could help people without being a doctor or nurse.

In Cape Girardeau, a college town, Nanci was in a high school that was on trimesters instead of semesters, and she had enough credits to graduate after her junior year. The summer before she started college she married Stan, a college roommate of her cousin. She had met Stan when her cousin brought him to her house. "I'm very lucky," she says. "Stan and I are soul mates. We sort of grew up together." When she was 17, Nanci had her son Randy, who is now 25.

Nanci started college right away, so she and Stan were both going to school and taking care of Randy. Fortunately, she says, she has never needed much sleep! Nanci studied biology, chemistry, and psychology in college in preparation for a career as a doctor. But in her last year of college, she thought, what happens if I don't get into medical school? She knew that many people are rejected the first time they apply. She remembered the nuclear medicine facility near the oncologist's office and decided to check out a career in nuclear medicine. When she learned more, she decided to train to be a nuclear medical technologist. After she graduated from college, she got into a one-year training program and then took a test to get her certification.

Kansas City Here I Come

Nanci didn't have any trouble finding a job after she got her certification as a CNMT (certified nuclear medical technologist). She went to Kansas City to visit some college friends and found that there were plenty of openings for technologists. The family moved to Kansas City and Nanci started in a hospital that had lots of older patients.

After five years, she accepted a very challenging job—she was asked to start a nuclear medicine program at Children's Mercy Hospital, which until that time had sent its patients to other hospitals to get the tests done. Nanci set up the policies and procedures for how things would be done. The work has always been interesting and challenging. "There is so much to learn. The changes in computer technology are changing the way nuclear medicine is practiced," she says. Nanci has been at the hospital 14 years now. When she started her career in the early 1980s, computers were much different than they are today.

When she isn't working or speaking about nuclear medicine to various groups of doctors and technologists, or serving her professional associations, Nanci is involved with her church. She used to teach Sunday School, but these days she just volunteers for the nursery occasionally and helps out with special projects. She also speaks to various clubs and civic groups about nuclear medicine and is listed in the speakers bureau of the Ronald McDonald House.

Telisha Royster

Telisha Royster

Telisha Royster, LPTA, contract work for Greater Southeast Hospital, Washington, DC, and for Manor Care Health Services, Arlington, VA

Associate's degree in Physical Therapist Assistant Program

Physical Therapist Assistant

She Gets Them Moving

When Telisha Royster talks about her work, her face lights up. Her work is physically demanding, emotionally draining, and wonderfully rewarding. "You are there to serve the patient. When you start with patients who can't lift their legs, and when they leave they are walking out the door, that's a wonderful sight."

Telisha is an LPTA, a licensed physical therapist assistant. She chooses to work part-time as a contract employee so she can have more time with her two small children and her husband. Usually, she works Saturdays at a nursing home and takes temporary assignments at a hospital,

PHYSICAL THERAPIST ASSISTANT

- $20,000 to $28,000

PHYSICAL THERAPIST

- $20,000 to $48,000

Source: *Encyclopedia of Careers and Vocational Guidance*. (1997). Chicago: J. G. Ferguson.

TELISHA'S CAREER PATH

Works at bakery,
▼ starts own
cake business

Building engineer
▼ (janitor) at newspaper,
meets Nathan

Researches her
▼ interests and
skills, volunteers
at hospital

sometimes as long as 6 months filling in for another therapist assistant who is on maternity leave.

Every Patient Different

Patients who are recovering from an operation such as knee surgery, an injury such as a broken ankle, or illness such as stroke need to do certain exercises to improve their ability to move the affected parts of the body. The physical therapist determines what treatment will help the individual and writes a plan. It is this plan that the physical therapist assistant follows as she works with the patient.

"I've been really blessed because of the therapists I work with. We have a good rapport. After you work with a therapist for a length of time, they become confident in your skills and know that you won't endanger the patient. The bottom line is the safety of the patient. A good relationship means having constant communication. Some therapists write an open-ended plan to start with a certain exercise, then add another, and see how the patient tolerates this weight or this particular movement. And I can make suggestions, like I think the patient might benefit from a certain exercise or another one. It makes for a wonderful working relationship."

On a typical day at the nursing home, Telisha arrives at 8 in the morning. Patient treatments don't start until 9, so this first hour may be

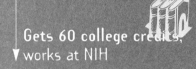

a time for a staff meeting or a scheduling meeting between the departments of physical therapy, occupational therapy, and speech therapy (so the patient isn't scheduled to be in two places at once). Or Telisha may have a "standup" meeting—all the disciplines get together and discuss how the patients are progressing. There are also conferences to give family members a progress report on their loved one.

If there are no meetings, Telisha may work on preparing billing. Or she may prepare progress reports

that are called SOAPs. Here's what the letters stand for—S, subjective, what the patient or family member might state; O, objective, what oc-

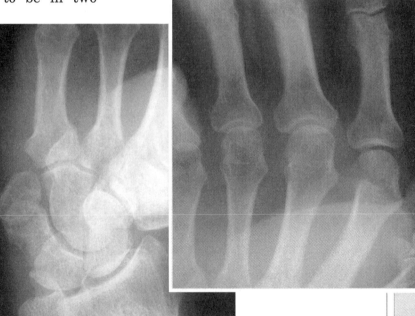

curred during a treatment session; A, the assessment; and P, the plan. These reports are to let everyone, including insur-

Graduates as ▼ LPTA, has daughter

Works two ▼ jobs part time

ance companies, know how the patient is progressing. They are quite detailed. For example: O might state must write a report on each patient once a week. In the hospital setting, Telisha must do the SOAP after each

> I enjoy what I do, but I get tired. It is physical work. Sometimes you have to lift a 250 pound person who is paralyzed.

that Mr. ABC is able to lift 2 pounds with his right leg and has increased to 5 pounds on his left leg. Telisha session with the patient. These are always hand-written notes. When Telisha works in the hospital, she uses a computer to request transportation of patients. The computer will tell her if there are any scheduling conflicts with other therapists, so she doesn't have to meet with them to do scheduling.

At the nursing home, Telisha may see 8 to 10 patients between 9 a.m. and 4:30 p.m. Sometimes she will go to the patients' rooms and bring them to the physical therapy department; other times an aide will transport them. Sometimes she will do "bedsides," doing some treatment exercises while the patient remains in bed. Each session is about 30 to 45 minutes long.

"I enjoy what I do, but I get tired. It is physical work. Sometimes you have to lift a 250 pound person who is paralyzed. You have supportive workers to help you, but you have to work to get that sliding board under the patients to move them to the mat."

Telisha's work is social, too. People like to talk. She listens and gets to know them. "If they can't do the exercises, it's emotional for them; they start crying. It's emotionally drain-

CAREER CHECKLIST ✔

You'll like this job if you ...

- Will do hard physical work
- Can be positive, a cheerleader
- Can work with people in pain
- Can follow directions, pay attention to details
- Are observant, understanding
- Can write well about your work

GROUNDBREAKERS

Segregation and Nurses

Public health nurses, funded by private and public monies, brought care to immigrant and working poor. In the United States, African Americans were barred from working in many white-run establishments, so they formed their own hospitals and offered training. In 1908, they created the National Association of Colored Graduate Nurses (AACGN). It was not until 1945 that army and navy nurse corps opened their doors to African American nurses and in 1948, the American Nursing Association opened its membership to people of color. Some three years later the AACGN disbanded. However, in 1971 for various reasons, nurses formed the National Black Nurses Association.

Source: *The Reader's Companion to Women's History.* (1998). NY: Houghton Mifflin

ing for me, but I'm the cheerleader. You have to keep them working through the pain, and everyone's tolerance to pain is different. You have to adapt every treatment session based on the needs and tolerance of the patient. I can look at their faces and know—someone needs to be pushed but another person might really be too tired and needs a little break."

Telisha gets an hour break for lunch, but sometimes it is shortened if sessions run overtime. She needs the break, but will do paper work on her lunch hour if she has fallen behind. After the last treatment of the day Telisha often has time to catch up on billing or SOAP notes. "I hate leaving stuff overnight."

A Long Career Search

Telisha is happy in her career. She worked many jobs to find what she really wanted to do, and then she worked hard to achieve it. Telisha

> When I was in those
> other careers
> and certain things started
> happening, I said
> 'I can't deal with this
> anymore' and I'd quit.
> Once I found what I really
> wanted to do, I stayed and
> dealt with it.

grew up in Washington, DC, and Clinton, Maryland. She always liked to work with her hands. In high school she was in the quantity foods program, which covered work involving preparation of large quantities of food. She was a cheerleader her senior year and also worked at McDonalds.

Telisha has two half-sisters, but she was an only child growing up in her mother's home. "I was always doing something. My mother had me in ballet, in tap, and lots of activities."

When Telisha graduated from high school she didn't know what she wanted to do. "I don't think they prepare you enough in school," she says. She took one class in accounting at the nearby community college, but didn't like it. Since she loved to decorate cakes, she took a job with a supermarket, training to be a baker's assistant. She liked it, and even started her own business selling decorated cakes to her church, friends, and family. But after a year, she decided to try something else. She thought about being a paralegal, and she thought about working for Bell Atlantic, where her mother and aunt worked. Then Telisha took a job as a building engineer (janitor) at the local newspaper plant, where she met her husband, Nathan, who is a foreman there. "The money was good, but I left because I knew I had more potential than being a clean-up person. So I took a job as a receptionist."

Telisha started new jobs thinking she would like them, but if something went differently than she expected, she would quit the job. She became frustrated that she could not find her niche, so Telisha went back to the community college. They offered a computer program to help students decide what they wanted to

> # I was always doing something. My mother had me in ballet, in tap, and lots of activities.

study. You answer all sorts of questions about what you like or what interests you. Then the computer

prints out careers you might like. Telisha decided she would research some of these careers. "I wanted to make sure that this time when I said I wanted to be something, I was going to go all the way to the end with it. I wasn't going to go in to study something I knew nothing about."

In the library, Telisha read books on medical careers. She contacted professional associations, and they sent her more information. In this way she narrowed the careers down to physician's assistant (PA) and physical therapist assistant (PTA). "Then I called the hospital and asked if I could volunteer, because I wanted to see what people in these jobs really did." For 6 months, Telisha worked her receptionist job during the week and on Saturdays she volunteered at the hospital.

The Big Decision

"I decided being a physical therapist was what I wanted to do, so I quit everything and started school. It was hard. I had a car loan to pay, but I didn't care. I had to take refresher courses in math and writing. Then I transferred to the University of Maryland to take all the courses required to get into the physical therapist program—biology, anatomy, and chemistry. I got a grant from my church, and my mother paid for my first semester. Then I got loans, and a part-time job in research at the National Institutes of Health (which paid my car loan)." By this time, Telisha was

engaged to Nathan, and he helped pay for her school. When she had completed the required prerequisite 60 credits to get into the physical therapist (bachelor's degree) program, they got married and moved into their home in Fort Washington, MD.

Telisha next applied to the PT programs at the University of Maryland Eastern Shore campus and Howard University. She didn't get in. (She later learned that you must reapply and reapply because they have lots of applicants and usually about 30 openings.) She then immediately applied for the physical therapist assistant program (associate's degree), but there were no openings at the time, so her name was on a waiting list.

Disappointed, Telisha went back to a receptionist/typist job, then soon became pregnant. She decided she wanted to stay home after her baby arrived, so she bought a computer and started a typing company. "I wrote a letter and sent it to different companies. I mainly targeted physical therapy businesses. I loved it because it let me stay home with my son, Pierre, and I was bringing in enough money to cover our food."

In the summer when Pierre was 3 months old, Northern Virginia Community College called and said she was accepted. "My husband said 'If you want to do this, I will support you.' It was hard. He would come home from his shift at work and I'd leave for school. He put up with my struggles. I kept one typing client and let the rest go."

Learning To Take Tests

Telisha found the PTA program hard, especially her beginning semester. "I knew the information, but I didn't know how to take tests." She asked for help from her professors. "The best advice I got was to outline my notes," she says. The college offered a test-taking lab, which Telisha took. "I started taking the tests twice, and I found that sometimes I'd misread the questions the first time. By the time I graduated my average was up from barely passing—69—to 80 and 90. I struggled and I feel honored in that. I thank God for that. Many times I thought, I cannot take this anymore. But I had conviction that this was what I wanted. I kept at it."

When Telisha's daughter, Nia Danyel, was born, Telisha was able to take the time she needed. She could adjust her work hours. She and Nathan enjoy spending their leisure time with the children and taking short trips to the nearby mountains and shore. They talk about taking a cruise, just the two of them, "sometime" in the future.

Sue Cowen

Sue Cowen

Sue Cowen, RD, Children's Memorial Hospital, Chicago, Il

Major in Home Economics, master's degree in Nutritional Science

Clinical
Dietitian

Her Kids Eat Right

Sue Cowen is a clinical dietitian at Children's Memorial Hospital in Chicago. She works closely with a doctor, a social worker, a medical psychologist, and a nurse. They work as a team to help children who have nutritional problems. The children might be underweight babies, children who suffer from eating disorders such as anorexia, kids who are overweight, or kids who are malnourished perhaps because of a congenital heart defect or other disease or sickness. Sue's job is to prescribe diets that will provide the children with the proper nutrition. She helps parents see that their kids are eating right.

Sue also works in a clinic for kids who have problems with constipation and other sicknesses of the intestines

DIETICIAN

Average $27,300 to $36,000

Source: *Encyclopedia of Careers and Vocational Guidance.* (1997). Chicago: J. G. Ferguson.

SUE'S CAREER PATH

Good grades,
▼ sews for friends
and family

Works at
▼ department
store

Graduates college

and stomach. In both her clinics, Sue's special role is to assess the child and educate the child and parents about nutrition, which will help the child grow properly. In the past, Sue worked in other areas in the hospital and helped children with diabetes, cancer and other diseases.

Figuring a Formula

Sue uses math skills every day to figure out such things as the calories, protein, vitamins, and minerals a child would need. For example, she might calculate how a baby would get the number of calories needed from a certain formula and write instructions for the parents so they can cre-

ate the formula at their home. She also has to be a very good communicator. She interviews the parent and often the child and counsels them both on how to make sure they get the proper nutrition. She also works closely with the doctors and makes recommendations about very special formulas and intravenous forms of nutrition.

The kids who come to the nutrition clinic can be referred by a doctor at the hospital. Sometimes their parents just bring them in because they are having problems. Sue likes working with the kids. "Kids don't care if you're a world class scientist or not. They just care that you care about them and treat them well," Sue says. "Also, they don't complain as much as adults." One advantage of working at a children's hospital is that you

can dress more casually. The atmosphere is friendly and relaxed.

Sue has to keep up with the latest information about nutrition. She often does research on the Internet and at university libraries to find out

instructions for parents and for preparing the talks she gives about nutrition. Sue also writes articles for dietitians, and she speaks on nutritional subjects to the doctors and nurses in the hospital and to other

There are lots of jobs available for dietitians. You could work for a food company, in health care, or in food service.

the latest thinking about diseases like diabetes that can be controlled with good diet. She uses a computer program to record and calculate body composition measurements, like how much fat a person has. And she uses the computer for word processing her

groups, like the PTA and service clubs.

Sue has worked at Children's Memorial Hospital for almost eight years. She was hired as the assistant director for clinical nutrition, a position that required her to create work

GROUNDBREAKERS

Nursing Pioneers at the Crimean War

Called the pioneer of modern nursing and medical hygiene, Florence Nightingale's (1820-1910) name is well known. An Englishwoman, she wanted to help during the Crimean War. Despite the open hostility of the male doctors, in 1854 she took a group of 28 nurses with her and cared for the wounded. Called the Lady of the Lamp, she returned to England and applied the principles of hygiene to public health work. She published *Notes on Nursing* in 1859. Queen Victoria appointed her to the Order of Merit, the first woman to be so honored.

Mary Seacole, a Jamaican nurse often called Mother or Aunty, established the British Hotel as a center for officers and soldiers in the Crimean War in 1856. She set it up at her own expense after the British army refused to help her. After the war, her many friends and benefactors helped her and paid her debts. She wrote of her experiences in *The Wonderful Adventures of Mrs. Seacole in Many Lands*, published in 1857.

Source: Irene M. Franck & David M. Bromstone. *(1995). Women's World.* NY: HarperCollins

schedules for the nutritionists who worked in the department and to perform administrative tasks such as reviewing the work of others. She also spent about one-third of her time doing clinical work. The director of Sue's department left and Sue was asked to be "acting director." As acting director, she was in charge of long-range planning, budgets, and forecasting future needs. But when the hospital was reorganized, as many hospitals were in the mid-1990s, management cut the number of managers by two-thirds. Her job was eliminated, and Sue had to decide whether to look for a job at another hospital or work full-time as a clinical nutritionist—actually doing the work rather than managing the people who did the work. She chose to stay at the hospital because she liked it there and wanted to work with the patients and their families.

A Big City Gal

Sue grew up in a Chicago suburb. Her father was an actuary (a type of accountant who works with pensions and retirement planning) and her mom stayed at home to take care of Sue and her older sister. Sue was a good student. School work was easy for her. She especially liked sewing class and home economics and even made her own winter coats. She also did sewing for her friends and family. During the summers she traveled all over the United States with her family on vacations.

At 16, Sue got a job in a department store as a clerk in the housewares department. "My father was always telling us to save money, so I knew how to manage money from a very early age," she says.

Sue went to Purdue University for a year, but she missed the big city, so after her first year she enrolled at Loyola University in Chicago and moved back home. She majored in home economics. Her curriculum included core sciences such as biology

CAREER CHECKLIST ✓

You'll like this job if you ...

Think food is important to good health

Are interested in math and science

Want to continue to learn

Like to work with children

Can explain nutrition concepts well

Work well on a team

Nutrition counseling should always be a part of health care. Children won't grow unless they are well-nourished; their wounds won't heal. We work on getting people to eat foods with the proper nutritional balance in moderate amounts.

and chemistry as well as cooking and sewing classes.

When Sue graduated from college, she worked for the Social Security Administration. "I was basically a paper pusher and I was bored," she says. Then she had a job as an assistant manager of a fabric store. Having access to beautiful material was great, but the hours were long and the pay was poor. So Sue decided to go back to school.

Sue got a master's degree in nutrition science, studying chemistry, biology, anatomy, and nutrition at Case Western Reserve University in Cleveland, Ohio. Her first job was in Akron, in a hospital's in-

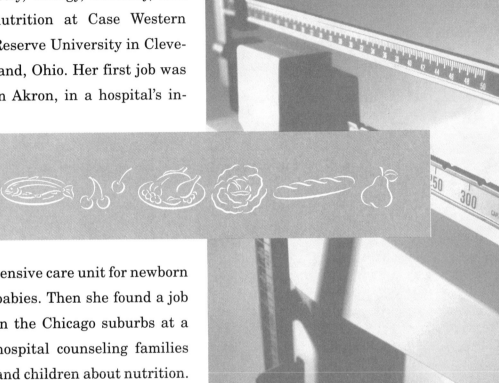

tensive care unit for newborn babies. Then she found a job in the Chicago suburbs at a hospital counseling families and children about nutrition. Later she got an even better job at Children's Memorial Hospital.

When she's not working, Sue enjoys gardening at her home in Skokie, 10 miles away from the hospital. She also likes to travel and to go to plays and movies with her friends.

Getting Started On Your

Own Career Path

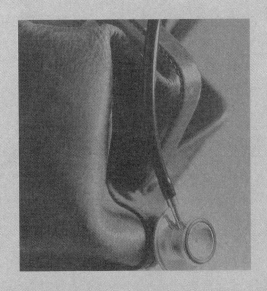

Getting Started On Your Own Career Path

WHAT TO DO NOW

To help you prepare for a career in health care, the women interviewed for this book recommend things you can do while in middle school, junior high, and high school.

Tiffany Osborn, emergency room physician

Make a decision that you want to be a doctor. Then wait until medical school to decide what kind of a doctor you want to be. How can you know until you've had a chance to experience some of the different specialties?

Nadine Eads, family nurse practitioner

Study math and science, and study English to hone your writing and speaking skills. And learn to type.

Shari Frishett, personal trainer and counselor

Play sports. This will show you your strength, and being physically strong will give you confidence. Think about studying exercise physiology in college or explore attending one of the few U.S. medical schools with an alternative medicine curriculum.

Nanci Burchell, nuclear medical technologist

Make sure you have good computer skills. Do some volunteer work. You can call the hospital and ask them to put you in touch with someone who is doing the type of work you're interested in. There are several ways to become a nuclear medical technologist. 1) You can get a BS degree in biology and chemistry and then take an extra year of training. 2) You can get a BS in nuclear medical technology, which requires that you specialize in this your last year in college. 3) You can take two years of radiology technologist training and an additional year of nuclear medical technology training right out of high school. Whichever way you go, you will need to take boards to get your certification. You can get certified by the Nuclear Medical Technologists Certifying Board or by the American Registry of Radiologic Technologists.

Telisha Royster, physical therapist assistant

You can get through the tough times if you have the drive, if it comes from within, and if you really want what you're going to school for.

Sue Cowen, clinical dietitian

You need to take the necessary classes so you can enter college. After college, you must pass a national test to be come accredited by the American Dietetics Association. In some states you also need to be licensed.

RECOMMENDED READING

Check the Biographies and History sections of your library for these books.

Those Extraordinary Blackwells by Elinor Rice Hays. (1967). New York: Harcourt Brace. (Elizabeth Blackwell, physician)

Margaret Sanger, Pioneer of the Future by Emily Taft Douglas. (1970). New York: Holt,Rinehart, & Winston. (Margaret Sanger, nurse)

Mary on Horseback: Three Mountain Stories by Rosemary Wells. (1998). New York: Dial Books for Young Readers. (Mary Breckinridge, nurse)

Young Clara Barton, Battlefield Nurse. (c1996). Mahwah, NJ: Troll Associations. (Clara Barton, nurse)

Protector of the Sick by Linda Carlson Johnson. (1991). New York: Blackbirch. (Mother Teresa)

Extraordinary Women of Medicine by Paulene R. Stille. (1977) New York: Children's Press.

Women in Medicine by Hedda Garza. (1994). New York: Franklin Watts.

PROFESSIONAL GROUPS

Many health specialties have their own organization and Web site. The groups below were selected because of their interest to women. Check these groups for career exploration information, local student chapters, scholarships, study guidelines. For additional organizations, check your library for the *Encyclopedia of Associations*, published by Gale Research.

General Women's Health

Boston Women's Book Collective
Libraries open to the public
240A Elm St., Somerville, MA 02164
(617) 625-0271; email bwhbc@igc.org

National Black Women's Health Project
175 Trinity Ave., SW, Atlanta, GA 30303
(404) 758-9590

National Women's Health Network
514 10th St., NW, Ste 400, Washington, DC 20004
(202) 347-1140

National Association of Professionals in Women's Health
175 W. Jackson Blvd., Ste 81711, Chicago, IL 60604-2801
(312) 786-1368
www.napwh.org

Physicians

American Medical Women (medical and osteopathic)
801 N. Fairfax, #400, Alexandria, VA 22314
(703) 838-0500

Association of Women Surgeons
414 Plaza Dr., Westmont, IL 60559
(630) 665-0392

Ruth Jackson Orthopaedic Society (surgeons)
6300 N. River Rd., #717, Rosemont, IL 60018-4226
(847) 698-1693

American Chiropractic Association

Student memberships, maintains library

> 1701 Clarendon Blvd., Arlington, VA 22209
>
> (703) 276-8800
>
> www.amerchiro.org

Women's Auxiliary of the International Chiropractors Association

Grants scholarships

> 1110 N. Glebe Rd., Ste 1000, Arlington, VA 22201
>
> (703) 528-5000

American Medical Association

Publishes *Journal of the American Medical Association (JAMA)*

> 515 N. State St., Chicago, IL 60610
>
> (312) 464-5000

Dentist

American Association of Women Dentists

Student memberships

> 401 N. Michigan Ave., Chicago, IL 60611-4267
>
> (312) 644-6610; email aawd@sba.com

Nurse

National Association for Practical Nurse Education and Service

> 1400 Silver Spring #310, Silver Spring, MD 20910
>
> (301) 588-2491

American Association of Colleges of Nursing

> One Dupont Circle, Washington, DC 20036
>
> (202) 463-6930

American Nurses Association

Maintains Hall of Fame

Sponsors American Academy of Nursing, which advances new concepts and proposes solutions to issues and problems confronting nurses and health Sponsors American

Nurses Foundation, which gives grants for research

    600 Maryland Ave., Ste 100, Washington, DC 20024-2571

    (202) 651-7000

    www.nursingworld.org

National Black Nurses Association

    1511 K St., NW #415, Washington DC 20005-1401

    (202) 393-6870

National League for Nursing

Accredits education programs and community agencies; keeps data on nursingservices

    61 Broadway, New York, NY 10006-4584

    (212) 989-9393

    www.nln.org

Association of Women's Health, Obstetric and Neonatal Nurses

    700 14th St. NW, #600, Washington, DC

    (202) 662-1608

Frontier Nursing

    Scholarships

    132 FNS Rd., Wendover, KY 41775

    (606) 672-2317

Visiting Nurse Association

    3801 E. Florida #900, Denver, CO 80210

    (303) 753-0218

Nurse Practitioner

American College of Nurse Practitioners

    503 Capitol Ct. NE #300, Washington, DC 20002

    (202) 546-4825; email acnp@nurse.org.

Nurse Midwife

Midwives Alliance of North America

 P.O. Box 175, Newton, KS 67114-0175

 (316) 283-4543

American College of Nurse-Midwives

 818 Connecticut Ave., Ste 900, Washington, DC 20006

 (202) 728-9860

 www.midwife.org

Physician's Assistant

American Academy of Physician Assistants

Scholarships, works with certifying organization, National Commission on Certification of Physician Assistants

 950 North Washington St., Alexandria, VA 22314-1552

 (703) 836-2272

 www.aapa.org

Nuclear Medicine

American Association for Women Radiologists

 1891 Preston White Dr., Reston, VA 20191-4397

 (703) 648-8939

 www.aawr.org

Society of Nuclear Medicine

 1850 Samuel Morse Dr., Reston, VA 20190

 (703) 708-9000

 www.snm.org

American Society of Radiologic Technologists

 15000 Central Ave. S.E., Albuquerque, NM 87123-3917

 (505) 298-4500

 www.asrt.org

Dietitian

American Dietetic Association

State groups, scholarships

216 West Jackson Blvd., Chicago, IL 60606

(312) 899-0040

www.eatright.org

American Society for Clinical Nutrition

Student members

9650 Rockville Pike, Bethesda, MD 20814-3998

(301) 530-7110

www.faseb.org/ascn

Alternative Medicine

Trends: Estimated expenditures for alternative medicine professional services increased 45.2% between 1990 and 1997 and were conservatively estimated at $21.2 billion in 1997, with at least $12.2 billion paid out of pocket (not covered by insurance). Use of alternative therapies increased for these principal conditions—back problems, allergies, arthritis, and digestive problems. Chiropractic, relaxation techniques, and massage therapy were among the therapies most commonly used. Therapies in use between 1990 and 1997 showing the largest increases were herbal medicine, massage, megavitamins, self-help groups, folk remedies, energy healing, and homeopathy.

> SOURCE: Eisenberg et al. (1998). Trends in Alternative Medicine Use in the United States, 1990-1997. *Journal of the American Medical Association* , 280, 1569–1571.

National Center for Homeopathy

Study groups, schools, and training programs

801 N. Fairfax St., Suite 306,Alexandria, VA 22314

(703) 548-7790

www.homeopathic.org

Naturopathy

These schools offer an accredited degree in naturopathy with extensive training in homeopathy:

Southwest College of Naturopathic Medicine

2140 East Broadway Rd., Tempe, AZ 85282

(602) 858-9100

www.scnm.edu

National College of Naturopathic Medicine

049 SW Porter St., Portland, OR 97201

(503) 499-4343

www.ncnm.edu

Bastyr University

14500 Juanita Dr. NE, Kenmore, WA 98028

(425) 823-1300

www.bastyr.edu

How COOL Are You?!

Cool girls like to DO things, not just sit around like couch potatoes. There are many things you can get involved in now to benefit your future. Some cool girls even know what careers they want (or think they want).

Not sure what you want to do? That's fine, too… the Cool Careers series can help you explore lots of careers with a number of great, easy to use tools! Learn where to go and to whom you should talk about different careers, as well as books to read and videos to see. Then, you're on the road to cool girl success!

Written especially for girls, this new series tells what it's like today for women in all types of jobs with special emphasis on nontraditional careers for women. The upbeat and informative pages provide answers to questions you want answered, such as:

✔ **What jobs do women find meaningful?**

✔ **What do women succeed at today?**

✔ **How did they prepare for these jobs?**

✔ **How did they find their job?**

✔ **What are their lives like?**

✔ **How do I find out more about this type of work?**

Each book profiles ten women who love their work. These women had dreams, but didn't always know what they wanted to be when they grew up. Zoologist Claudia Luke knew she wanted to work outdoors and that she was interested in animals, but she didn't even know what a zoologist was, much less what they did and how you got to be one. Elizabeth Gruben was going to be a lawyer until she discovered the world of Silicon Valley computers and started her own multimedia company. Mary Beth Quin grew up in Stowe, Vermont, where she skied competitively and taught skiing. Now she runs a ski school at a Virginia ski resort. These three women's stories appear with others in a new series of career books for young readers.

The Cool Careers for Girls series encourages career exploration and broadens girls' career horizons. It shows girls what it takes to succeed, by providing easy-to-read information about careers that young girls may not have considered because they didn't know about them. They learn from women who are in today's workplace—women who know what it takes today to get the job.

ORDER FORM

Title	Paper	Cloth	Quantity
Cool Careers for Girls in Computers	$12.95	$19.95	_____
Cool Careers for Girls in Sports	$12.95	$19.95	_____
Cool Careers for Girls with Animals	$12.95	$19.95	_____
Cool Careers for Girls in Health (June 1999)	$12.95	$19.95	_____
Cool Careers for Girls in Engineering (July 1999)	$12.95	$19.95	_____
Cool Careers for Girls with Food (August 1999)	$12.95	$19.95	_____
		SUBTOTAL	_____

VA Residents add 4½ % sales tax _____

Shipping/handling $5.00+ $5.00

$1.50 for each additional book order (__ x $1.50) _____

      TOTAL ENCLOSED _____

SHIP TO: (street address only for UPS or RPS delivery)
Name: _____
Address: _____

☐ I enclose check/money order for $ ___ made payable to Impact Publications
☐ Charge $_____ to: ☐ Visa ☐ MasterCard ☐ AmEx ☐ Discover

Card #: _____ Expiration: _____
Signature: _____ Phone number: _____

Phone toll-free at 1-800/361-1055, or fax/mail/email your order to:
Impact Publications
9104-N Manassas Drive, Manassas Park, VA 20111-5211
Fax: 703/335-9486; email: orders@impactpublications.com